CHARACTERS

A one-year exploration of the Bible
through the lives of its people.

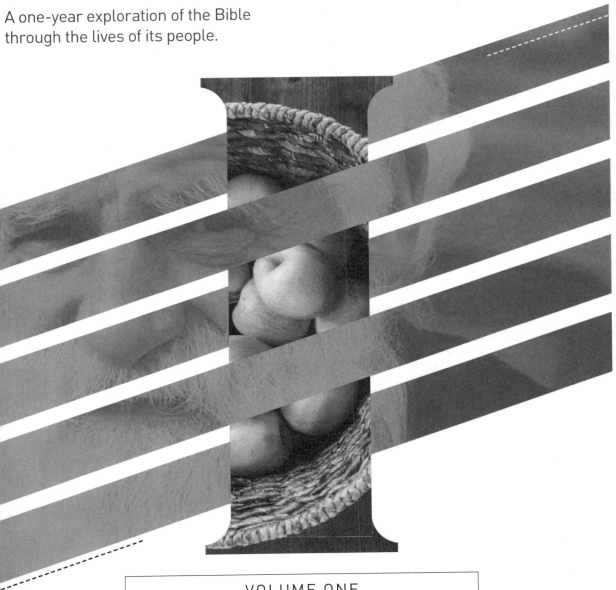

VOLUME ONE

The Patriarchs

LifeWay Press® • Nashville, Tennessee

EDITORIAL TEAM

Brandon Hiltibidal
Director, Discipleship and Groups Ministry

Brian Daniel
Manager, Short-Term Discipleship

Joel Polk
Editorial Team Leader

Michael Kelley
Content Developer

David Briscoe
Content Developer

G.B. Howell Jr.
Content Developer

Rob Tims
Content Editor

Laura Magness
Content Editor

Gena Rogers
Production Editor

Darin Clark
Art Director

Denise Wells
Designer

Lauren Rives
Designer

From the creators of *Explore the Bible, Explore the Bible: Characters* is a seven-volume resource that examines the lives of biblical characters within the historical, cultural, and biblical context of Scripture. Each six-session volume includes videos to help your group understand the way each character fits into the storyline of the Bible.

ISBN 978-1-4300-7034-4 • Item 005823502
Dewey decimal classification: 220.92
Subject headings: BIBLE. O.T.--BIOGRAPHY / PATRIARCHS (BIBLE)

We believe that the Bible has God for its author; salvation for its end; and truth, without any mixture of error, for its matter and that all Scripture is totally true and trustworthy. To review LifeWay's doctrinal guideline, please visit lifeway.com/doctrinalguideline.

Scripture quotations are taken from the Christian Standard Bible®, Copyright © 2017 by Holman Bible Publishers. Used by permission. Christian Standard Bible® and CSB® are federally registered trademarks of Holman Bible Publishers.

To order additional copies of this resource, write to LifeWay Resources Customer Service; One LifeWay Plaza; Nashville, TN 37234; fax 615-251-5933; call toll free 800-458-2772; or order online at LifeWay.com; email orderentry@lifeway.com.

Printed in the United States of America

Groups Ministry Publishing • LifeWay Resources
One LifeWay Plaza • Nashville, TN 37234

CONTENTS

ABOUT EXPLORE THE BIBLE

The Whole Truth, Book by Book

Explore the Bible is an ongoing family of Bible study resources that guides the whole church through the only source of the truth on which we can rely: God's Word. Each session frames Scripture with biblical and historical context vital to understanding its original intent, and unpacks the transforming truth of God's Word in a manner that is practical, age-appropriate, and repeatable over a lifetime.

Find out more at goExploreTheBible.com.

HOW TO USE THIS STUDY

This Bible study includes six sessions of content for group and personal study. Regardless of what day of the week your group meets, each session begins with group study. Each group session utilizes the following elements to facilitate simple yet meaningful interaction among group members and with God's Word.

INTRODUCTION

This page includes introductory content and questions to get the conversation started each time your group meets.

GROUP DISCUSSION

Each session has a corresponding teaching video to introduce the story. These videos have been created specifically to teach the group more about the biblical figure being studied. After watching the video, continue the group discussion by reading the Scripture passages and discussing the questions that follow. Finally, conclude each group session with a time of prayer, reflecting on what you discussed.

BIOGRAPHY AND FURTHER INSIGHT MOMENT

These sections provide more in-depth information regarding the biblical character being spotlighted each session and can be included in the group discussion or personal study times.

PERSONAL STUDY

Three personal studies are provided for each session to take individuals deeper into Scripture and to supplement the content introduced in the group study. With biblical teaching and introspective questions, these sections challenge individuals to grow in their understanding of God's Word and to respond in faith.

LEADER GUIDE

A tear out leader guide for each session is provided on pages 95-106. This section also includes sample answers or discussion prompts to help you jump start or steer the conversation.

VOLUME ONE

The Patriarchs

ADAM
AND EVE
The First Humans

INTRODUCTION

What is the meaning of life?

To find the true answer to this question, we have to go back to the very beginning when life began. Only through knowing where we came from can we know who we are, where we are going, and why we are here at all. At the beginning, we find the Book of Genesis, the first book of the Bible, which documents human history and beginnings in Mesopotamia. Genesis focuses on God's perfect creation of the world and its inhabitants, including many key figures of the Old Testament.

In the beginning, God and God alone existed. Genesis 1 and 2 record God's creative process, speaking into existence from nothing all that we see and know. After each act of creation, God reflected on His work and declared, "It is good." From God came everything else in creation, including the first human beings, Adam and Eve. Unlike everything else in creation, Adam and Eve were created "in the image of God." Having created Adam and Eve, God declared His creation to be "very good."

How does knowing where we come from help us answer the question of the meaning of life?

In your own words, describe the world of Adam and Eve before they sinned against God.

Watch the video teaching for Session 1 to discover "The World of Adam and Eve," then continue the group discussion.

GROUP DISCUSSION

FOCUS ATTENTION

Share some ways in which you are creative. How does this kind of creativity imitate God's creativity? How is it different from God's ability?

EXPLORE THE TEXT

As a group, read Genesis 1:1-5.

How is God's authority on display in these verses?

What attributes of God can we identify from the fact that He existed before the universe was created?

As a group, read Genesis 1:27.

How does the creation of man and woman in verse 27 speak to the inherent worth of every person?

As a group, read Genesis 3:1-7.

What lies about God did Satan speak to Eve? Why do you think these lies are easy to believe and repeat?

What do you think Adam and Eve hoped to gain by eating the fruit, despite God's instruction to avoid it?

As a group, read Genesis 3:14-19.

Sin must be judged because God is holy. How did God curse the serpent? Adam and Eve? How do you see evidence of these consequences today?

APPLY THE TEXT

God demonstrated His power by creating the universe with purpose simply by speaking it into existence. He made human beings in His image with the capacity to love and worship Him. He gave humanity the blessing of governing the earth in His stead, and He set apart a holy day for rest and refreshment.

Why is the story of creation central to a strong biblical worldview?

In what ways does the belief that God created humanity in His image impact your outlook on life?

How have you seen the sanctity of human life violated in the world today? What practical steps can you take to affirm that all people are made in God's image and are worthy of respect?

Close your group time in prayer, reflecting on what you have discussed.

ADAM AND EVE

KEY VERSES

So God created man in his own image; he created him in the image of God; he created them male and female. God blessed them, and God said to them, "Be fruitful, multiply, fill the earth, and subdue it."

— Genesis 1:27-28a

BASIC FACTS

1. Name *Adam* possibly means "to be red or ruddy"; related to the Hebrew word for "ground, land."

2. Name *Eve* probably means "living"; called "the mother of all the living" (Gen. 3:20).

3. No human parents; created directly by God.

4. Lived in the garden of Eden (location uncertain) until driven out by God as a result of their sin.

5. Adam lived to age 930; Eve's age at death is unknown.

TIMELINE

CREATION

- Day 1: Light and darkness created
- Day 2: Atmosphere/sky created
- Day 3: Dry ground and plants created
- Day 4: Sun, moon, and stars created
- Day 5: Birds and sea animals created
- Day 6: Land animals and humans created
- Day 7: The Lord rested—Sabbath

PRE-4000 BC

- Sin introduced
- Cain and Abel born; Abel murdered
- Seth born

KNOWN FOR

1. Adam and Eve were the first human beings; they were created as male and female in God's image (Gen. 1:27).

2. Adam gave names to all the wild animals and birds God created (Gen. 2:19).

3. Adam and Eve were the first man and woman to be married and give birth to children (Gen. 2:24; 4:1-2,25).

4. They introduced sin and its consequences into the human race (Gen. 3:6,16-19); Adam bequeathed the "sin nature" to all human descendants (Rom. 5:12).

5. Adam and Eve were the first to cultivate food in a garden (Gen. 2:15).

6. They were also the first to face temptation from the devil (Gen. 3:6).

7. They were the first to lose a child to violent crime (Gen. 4:8).

8. Adam and Eve were cast out of the garden of Eden to work the ground (Gen. 3:23).

4000–2100 BC

- Worldwide flood 2350
- Tower of Babel 2250
- Job 2100–1900
- Abraham 2166–1991

2000 BC

- God's covenant with Abraham 2081
- Ishmael born 2080
- Isaac 2066–1886
- Jacob 2006–1859

God "Created": A Word Study

The opinions by Christians about how and when God created the universe vary. Young Earth Creationists believe the universe is likely 6,000 to 10,000 years old and reject evolution as an explanation for the human species. Old Earth Creationists generally hold that the earth is billions of years old, and they also reject evolution. Those who affirm Intelligent Design would argue that scientific evidence supports the belief in a Creator God. While all Christians may not agree on the details of how God created the universe, all believers agree that He is the Creator of it all. The Hebrew word to express creation first occurs in Genesis 1:1 and is the word *bara'*. The term *bara'* is unique in that it "emphasizes the initiation of [an] object."[1]

God's Initial Work of Creation

Genesis 1:1 says, "In the beginning God created the heavens and the earth."[2] God is always the subject of this Hebrew verb when it means "create." The first chapter of Genesis uses the verb *bara'* in only three verses. In Genesis 1:1, the context indicates God created the universe *ex nihilo* or "out of nothing." Such action is beyond human capabilities. Other passages also affirm creation as *ex nihilo* (see Heb. 11:3; compare Ps. 33:6,9; Col. 1:16).

The next two usages of the word *bara'* in Genesis 1 highlight the creation of life, both animal and human life. Genesis 1:21 highlights the creation of animal life. Likewise, Genesis 1:27 says, "So God created man in His own image; He created him in the image of God; He created them male and female."

The use of *bara'* with reference to the creation of man indicates the special value that God places on humanity. In fact, man is the Lord's highest creation, for man is created in His image. God formed (created) man from the dust of the earth (see Gen. 2:7)—a clear indication that *bara'* in this instance does not mean to create out of nothing.

T. Van McClain, "God 'Created': A Word Study," *Biblical Illustrator*, Summer 2013.

Ancient Babylonian creation epic. In this story, Anshar, the god of the celestial world, summons other gods to celebrate the Babylonian god Marduk who has defeated Tiamat, the embodiment of primeval Chaos. The story also tells how Marduk used Tiamat's carcass to form heaven and earth. The tall narrow shape is characteristic of tablets in this series.

Illustrator Photo/ British Museum, London (31/9/67)

Illustrator Photo/Louise Kohl Smith (33/36/12)

Overlooking the ruins at the ancient site of Ebla (now called Tel Mardikh) in modern northwest Syria. In the 1970s, archaeologists unearthed thousands of tablets inscribed with details of everyday life in the city of Ebla late in the third millennium BC. Written in Sumerian script, the tablets contain many of the same names of people and places that are in the Old Testament, plus stories that are similar to the biblical accounts of the flood, the tower of Babel, and creation. However, the people of Ebla did not know or worship Yahweh. Instead, they worshiped several gods, including Dagan, Ishtar, Enki, Ninki, and others.

1. Thomas E. McComiskey, "ar'B'" (bara', to create) in *Theological Wordbook of the Old Testament*, ed. R. Laird Harris (Chicago: Moody Press, 1980), 1:127.
2. Unless otherwise indicated, all Scripture quotations are from the Christian Standard Bible (CSB).

Read Genesis 1:26-31.

God spoke the universe into existence out of nothing. Unlike some creation myths that involve unusual creatures and cosmic struggles, Genesis presents one God who spoke creation into being and who still controls His creation. His creation was orderly, purposeful, and powerful. By reading the creation account, we begin to learn just who this God is who still rules over His creation.

This is especially true in His creation of mankind, which is introduced in a warm, personal conversation involving the three Persons of the Trinity: "Let us make man in our image, according to our likeness" (v. 26).

What does it mean to be created in God's image? It doesn't mean that human beings have a divine nature or can someday become gods. Instead, it means that God made us to resemble Him in ways that no other parts of creation do. Adam had the capacity to know and worship God perfectly.

If we keep going into Genesis 2, we see that it was not good for man to be alone. God created Eve, also in His image, and because both men and women bear the image of God, they are equal in dignity and worth to Him.

What is the best thing to you about being made in God's image?

What do you think life was like for Adam and Eve? How would their relationship have been different than our relationships today?

Adam and Eve began their existence in perfect harmony with God, with creation, and with each other. They tended the garden, and their work was a joy. God commanded them not only to tend the garden, but to have children and fill the earth with human beings (see v. 22). Like any divine benefit, the gift of human sexuality is meant for our good.

God also gave Adam and Eve the responsibility of governing the earth as His representatives. As stewards of this amazing planet, we are to promote its well-being, including the well-being of all of its inhabitants and resources. Every living thing must have nourishment to survive, grow, and reproduce. God therefore gave humanity and all the wildlife of the earth access to the vegetation He created (see 1:11). Adam and Eve were vegetarians, for it was not until after the worldwide flood in Noah's day that the Lord gave human beings the additional benefit of eating meat and fish (see Gen. 9:2-3).

What are some ways believers can practice and promote good stewardship of God's creation? What role does thanking God for the provision He has made for our well-being play in this stewardship?

When God surveyed the totality of His creative work, He declared that it was "very good indeed" (v. 31). Everything that was good, beneficial, and purposeful for His creation was in place and in harmony.

Read Genesis 2:4-9,15-18.

Adam and Eve were unique among all God's creation. To emphasize this, Moses used a different name for God in Genesis 2 than in Genesis 1. In Genesis 1, the English name "God" translates the Hebrew term *Elohim* [EL oh heem]. In 2:4, Moses used the name *Yahweh Elohim*, which is written in English as "the LORD God." *Yahweh* is God's personal, covenant name that He revealed to Moses at the burning bush; it means "I am" (see Ex. 3:13-15). Together, the two names emphasize that the all-powerful God who created the world also related to humanity in a personal way.

These verses also show the deep connections God wove into His world. The two human beings needed a place to live, work, and fulfill their God-given purpose. The world needed human beings to cultivate and care for it. God prepared the earth first, and then He made its caretakers.

God created out of nothing the materials He used to fashion human beings. Indeed, the Hebrew words translated "the man" and "the ground" are related. The picture is that of a skilled potter taking up a mound of clay in his hands and shaping it into a marvelous vessel. Even so, God fashioned the first man's body of the dust of the ground (see Ps. 103:14). This was a "hands-on" process. The language in Genesis 2 shows us something of God's personal and intimate creation of Adam and Eve, telling us that He fashioned the physical body, and then He "breathed the breath of life . . . into the man" (Gen. 2:7), later called "Adam." This special action set human beings apart from all other creatures. When God's breath entered into the man's nostrils, Adam became a living soul capable of relating personally with his Creator.

How can these verses encourage someone who feels insignificant?

God put the man in the garden to live in and enjoy. However, the garden was never intended to be a place of idleness or self-indulgence. Rather, God expected the man to make the garden productive and to manage it wisely—key aspects of ruling over the earth in God's stead. Human life has a God-given purpose. Important aspects of that purpose involve being productive and being good stewards of God's creation.

How can we honor God through our work? How is being productive an extension of the wise stewardship of God's creation?

God knew that it was not good for Adam to be alone. Companionship and intimacy are essential to human happiness, enjoyment, and fulfillment. Loneliness is not always caused by an absence of other people. It can also be the result of a lack of meaningful relationships. God wants people to live in mutually fulfilling relationships.

How does God use relationships to enrich our lives? What does our need for relationships reveal about our need for God?

Genesis 1:27 states simply that God created mankind as "male and female." In 2:21-25, Moses described in greater detail the amazing surgery God performed to give Adam a helper. God put the man into a deep sleep, removed a rib from his side, and used the rib to fashion a woman, later called "Eve" (see 3:20). Adam immediately acknowledged that the woman was his perfect counterpart. God also used the moment to establish the sacred bond of marriage between the man and the woman. Adam and Eve had a wonderful place to live and work. Now they could join together without shame in establishing a home and family. All was as God intended it to be. But all of that was about to change.

Read Genesis 3:1-7,14-19.

A new character pops up in Adam and Eve's story in Genesis 3—the serpent. In this case, the serpent was being used by another being, an evil being whose desire was to tempt, accuse, and destroy every good thing God had made, especially human beings.

The serpent asked Eve a simple question, but one that was carefully designed to raise doubts about God. Eve likely felt that to answer "yes" was to falsely accuse God of being stingy, untruthful, and unloving. To answer "no" was to suggest that it must be okay to eat fruit even from the tree of the knowledge of good and evil.

To her credit, Eve corrected the serpent's deceptive question. Adam and Eve had God's permission to eat from all of the trees in the garden except one, the tree in the middle. Interestingly, Eve added that she and Adam were forbidden to touch the tree of the knowledge of good and evil, lest they die. While God's specific command was that they were not to eat from the tree (see Gen. 2:17), perhaps the couple had agreed that not touching it was an even stronger safeguard against disobedience.

The serpent changed tactics, moving from planting doubts about God's goodness to openly questioning God's integrity. The "father of lies" (John 8:44) accused God of lying to the man and woman about the consequences of sin. The serpent insisted that God's warning about sin was intentionally misleading. God was holding out on them. These are still the arguments Satan makes today—that God isn't good, loving, and generous, and that true satisfaction can be found apart from Him.

Knowing how Satan operates, what are some things people can do to recognize and resist temptation?

Satan never directly told Eve to disobey God. He simply clouded her mind with doubt and then watched as an internal struggle took over. Eve looked at the forbidden tree in a different way. It no longer seemed off-limits or dangerous; instead it looked pleasant and seemed to be a source of wisdom. Eve took fruit from the forbidden tree and ate. Then she gave some to Adam and he also ate, and the perfect harmony for which they had been created was broken.

As the serpent promised, the man's and woman's eyes were opened. What they gained, however, was not a God-like knowledge but rather a sense of deep guilt and shame. They became self-conscious of their nakedness. In a futile attempt to hide their shame and guilt, they sewed fig leaves together to wear as coverings. They had lost their innocence. Life would not be the same again.

Why do you think people so often try to hide their sins? What do Acts 2:38 and 1 John 1:9 teach us to do instead of hiding our sins?

Sin entered the world, and being just, God pronounced His judgment on all involved— first on the serpent, then on the woman, and finally on the man. But even in the midst of judgment, God showed His grace. God's words to the serpent were also a declaration of war against Satan. These verses are also the Bible's first prophetic glimpse of the good news that would come in Jesus Christ. Christ defeated Satan by His death and resurrection. Although the battle continues for believers until Christ's return, our victory over sin and death is guaranteed through Christ (see Rev. 5:5-10).

Adam and Eve would one day return to dust. Physical death had entered the human experience.

In what ways do you see the consequences of humanity's fall ongoing in today's world? In what ways is God's mercy evident?

NOAH

The Lone Righteous Man

INTRODUCTION

As Genesis continues, we see that Adam and Eve obeyed God's command to multiply and fill the earth. But unlike them, every human born after them was born with a heart bent toward sin. Things went from bad to worse.

Human beings fell into an ever-worsening pattern of sin. The serpent promised Adam and Eve they would become more like God, yet they became more like the one they believed. Human beings became more and more ungodly. In the midst of this wickedness we meet Noah.

Noah lived in what may have been the most corrupt period in human history. By the time Noah was born, the earth was so filled with evil that God decided He would flood the earth and start over. God would save a remnant—Noah and his family—to repopulate the earth and begin anew.

Noah's story is a story of faith. It's the portrait of a man who believed God, despite all the evidence to the contrary. The faith of Noah is a real faith, one that resulted in real action. Like all real faith, Noah's led to blessing.

When have you seen things go from bad to worse as a result of sin?

When you think of the story of Noah, does anything about the story surprise you? Explain.

Watch the video teaching for Session 2 to discover "The World of Noah," then continue the group discussion.

FOCUS ATTENTION

Summarize the story of Noah in one word. What does this man's experience teach us about God?

EXPLORE THE TEXT

As a group, read Genesis 6:11-13.

How does God's judgment on sinful humanity during the days of Noah cause you to view the evil and corruption in our world today? How does it cause you to view God?

In what ways can considering God's judgment help us see His mercy more clearly?

As a group, read Genesis 6:14-18.

What beliefs did Noah indicate by his obedience to God?

How is obedience to God different today than it was for Noah?

How do the two promises in verse 18 relate to the rest of humanity and creation, beyond Noah's family?

As a group, read Genesis 7:7-14.

What does it mean to you that God keeps His Word, both in mercy and in judgment? What does this truth say about His character?

APPLY THE TEXT

In the midst of all the wickedness that filled the earth, God took notice of Noah. Noah was a righteous and blameless man who sought to please God and to walk with Him. God told Noah of His plan to wipe all flesh from the earth with the exception of him and his family. He told Noah to build an ark, the vessel that would preserve him and his family from the coming judgment. By faith, Noah trusted God and spent the next 120 years constructing the ark. During that period, God gave the world ample opportunities to repent. The world, however, refused Noah's witness.

What message does the account of Noah have for us today regarding obedience? The seriousness of sin? God's mercy? The importance of guarding and cultivating our hearts and the hearts of our family members?

What must Noah have been confident of regarding God in order to practice this kind of obedience?

How could that kind of confidence change the way you live in a practical way?

Close your group time in prayer, reflecting on what you have discussed.

NOAH

KEY VERSE

Then the LORD said to Noah, "Enter the ark, you and all your household, for I have seen that you alone are righteous before me in this generation."

— Genesis 7:1

BASIC FACTS

1. Name *Noah* is of uncertain meaning; possibly related to a verb meaning "to rest" or "comfort, relief" (based on Noah's father stating that his son would bring relief from God's curse on the ground).

2. Son of Lamech [LAY mek]; grandson of Methuselah [mih THOOZ uh luh], the longest living man in Scripture at 969 years.

3. Noah's wife's name is unknown; two later Jewish rabbinical sources list her name as Naamah [NAY uh muh].

4. Fathered Shem, Ham, and Japheth [JAY feth]; all were born after Noah was 500 years old.

5. Lived a total of 950 years.

TIMELINE

4000–2000 BC
Noah 2950
Worldwide flood 2350
Tower of Babel built 2250
Job 2100?–1900
Abraham 2166–1991

2000–1900 BC
Isaac 2066–1886
Jacob 2006–1859
Twelfth Dynasty of Egypt 1991–1786
Chinese create first zoo 2000
Code of medical ethics in Mesopotamia 2000
Babylonians, Egyptians divide days into hours, minutes, and seconds 2000

KNOWN FOR

1. Noah stood out as the only man of his generation who lived in right relationship with God (Gen. 6:9). He and his family lived during a time of unimaginable wickedness, leading God to regret having created humanity (vv. 5-6) and deciding to destroy all creatures on the earth with a flood (vv. 13,17).

2. God made a covenant with Noah to save his family, preserve pairs of creatures through the ark, and repopulate the earth after the flood (vv. 17-22).

3. Noah was 600 years old when the flood began (7:6,11). Torrential rain continued for forty days, covering all the earth and destroying all living things not in the ark (vv. 17-20). After five months, the floodwaters began to recede so that by the seventh month, the ark came to rest in the mountain range of Ararat [EHR uh rat] (8:3-4). In total, Noah and his family spent approximately one year on the ark (vv. 13-19).

4. Since all other human beings on earth were destroyed in the flood, Noah's three sons are the male ancestors of all human beings alive today, including those who built the tower of Babel at Shinar (11:1-9).

5. After the flood, Noah worshiped the Lord, building an altar and sacrificing burnt offerings. God declared a covenant with Noah signified by a rainbow (9:12-13), promising never again to curse the ground because of human wickedness (8:21).

6. Noah showed later in his life that the sin nature had not been destroyed by the flood when he became drunk and exposed himself shamefully to his sons (vv. 20-27). A future sacrifice would be required to break the curse of mankind's sin (Heb. 10:8-10).

1900–1800 BC

- Potter's wheel introduced to Crete 1900
- Use of sails on boats in the Aegean 1900
- Mesopotamians discover what later became known as Pythagorean theorem 1900
- Joseph sold into Egypt 1898
- Jacob and family move to Egypt 1876

1800–1700 BC

- Musical theory developed in Mesopotamia 1800
- Multiplication tables developed in Mesopotamia 1800
- Babylonians develop catalog of stars and planets 1800
- Horses introduced in Egypt 1800

Noah's Life and Times

By Scott Langston

What were society and culture like in Noah's day? Genesis 6–9 provides various snapshots, but each portrayal depicts society as wicked. As a prelude to the flood account, Genesis 6:1-8 records the strange story of the sons of God taking the daughters of man for wives and producing a people known as "the powerful men of old, the famous men" (v. 4). This passage establishes how evil society had become; it also introduces why God sent a flood to wipe out sinful humanity.

Genesis 6:5-8 contrasts the goodness of God's creation with the evil that had filled it. The people were exceedingly wicked, with every thought constantly inclined toward evil (Gen. 6:5).

Genesis 6:11-13 depicts society as corrupt or, literally, ruined. This ruining was connected to the people's violence (see vv. 11,13). God determined He was going to destroy, or ruin, the earth and all humanity.

Noah was a righteous man (see v. 9); he did not share society's values or actions. He was "blameless" in his generation—meaning he was "complete, whole, sound, innocent."[1] Because of his lifestyle, Noah was described as walking with God, a description used elsewhere only of Enoch (see 5:22,24). Preparing for the flood, Noah faithfully carried out all of God's instructions. The Bible says that he alone was righteous (see 7:1). Fittingly, since only Noah obeyed God, only Noah and his family survived the flood.

Yet the flood did not cure the world of sin. Some time after the flood, Noah became drunk and lay naked (see 9:20-29). Scripture does not focus on Noah's drunkenness, but instead emphasizes the actions of Ham, Noah's son. Ham, who did not cover up his father, but went and told his brothers, is denounced. His brothers covered their father; they subsequently were blessed, while Ham's descendants were cursed.

Without providing many details of Noah's life and society, his story spotlights God's judgment and mercy. It also demonstrates the difference a godly person can make in an ungodly world. Noah's story remains relevant, even in today's world.

1. Gordan Wenham, *Word Biblical Commentary: Genesis 1–15* (Waco: Word Books, 1987), 1071.

Scott Langston, "Noah's Life and Times," *Biblical Illustrator*, Summer 1999..

In the distance, the snow-capped peak of
Mount Ararat rises to a height of 16,940 feet.
Ararat is the tallest peak in modern Turkey.
According to Scripture, Noah's ark came to rest
on Mount Ararat as the floodwaters receded.

Illustrator Photo/ Bob Schatz
(25/20/6) or (25/20/15)

Overview of the western
segment of Ugarit, which
was a Canaanite port city
located in what is now Syria.
Ancient texts discovered
at Ugarit reflected many
details found in Scripture;
one specifically enlightens
the Bible's condemnation
of Ham.

Illustrator Photo/ James McLemore
(21/20/13)

29

Read Genesis 6:11-17.

It's remarkable to see what happened to the earth in the span of a few chapters. But that's the way of sin—it always starts small and leads to something more. By the time we get to Genesis 6, the single spark of Adam and Eve's sin became a wildfire.

The Bible vividly describes those days, saying that people thought of "nothing but evil all the time" (v. 5). Imagine living in such a time. Imagine being surrounded by corruption. Imagine the self-centeredness, the greed, and the violence. In such a society, Noah stood apart. Noah was marked by faith, not wickedness. But that faith would be tested if Noah was to do what God commanded. And what a command it would be.

Put yourself in Noah's place. How do you think you would have reacted if God commanded you to build an ark?

God was specific in His instructions. The type of wood was probably pine or cypress, commonly used in ship building. Because it would house animals, God commanded Noah to build rooms and waterproof them. According to the dimensions, the ark was a box-like vessel designed for flotation instead of navigation. The size of this vessel was enormous by ancient standards. The ark would have been about half the length of a ship the size of the Titanic. The boxy design maximized the interior space and provided adequate room for Noah, his entire family, and all the animals with them.

The ark had lower, middle, and upper decks to house the animals as well as Noah and his family. The vessel was well-ventilated all the way around under the roof line—an important consideration because of all of the animals on board. This gap also allowed natural light to filter into the upper deck.

A single door was the only entrance and exit. The door was important to provide an entry point before the flood and an exit point to the land after the flood. When the rains came and Noah and his family were safely aboard the ark, God Himself shut the door (see 7:16). In many ways, the ark is a reflection of the characteristics of Christ. Like the single door on the ark, Jesus referred to Himself as "the gate for the sheep" (John 10:7), as well as the only way to the Father (see John 14:6). Just as God provided the ark to save Noah and his family, God made provision for salvation through Jesus Christ for all who believe and take refuge in Him.

What does Noah's undertaking of such a big project tell you about his faith in God? How would you describe the relationship between God's promises and Noah's faith?

One hundred and twenty years. Imagine it. Noah likely spent as many as 120 years building the ark (see v. 3). Throughout those years, Noah remained steadfast to the task, because he had faith that what God told him about the coming deluge was true (see Heb. 11:7). But imagine, too, how it must have felt when the rain began to fall.

In one sense, it must have been gratifying for Noah to see the fulfillment of God's promises. He waited; he remained faithful. He worked in obedience for more than a century, and he was going to bear witness to God's own faithfulness. At the same time, however, imagine the sense of mourning he likely felt to see this great judgment come to pass.

In a way, it's the same with us. We remain faithful to God, believing He will keep His promises. Even so, we also mourn as we see others around us continue to go their own way despite the judgment of God that is still to come.

Read Genesis 6:18; 7:11-14.

God revealed His plan to Noah. He was going to destroy, through a great flood, every living, breathing creature—including humans, animals, and birds. This deluge was God's judgment on the evil that had completely saturated and corrupted the earth. When the floodwaters finally came, they confirmed Noah's faith as well as his faithfulness in following God's instructions.

Then Noah experienced something no human ever had before. For the first time in human history, God established a covenant with a man. A covenant is a solemn agreement between two parties in which each party is under obligation to perform his part. Covenants generally included conditions, benefits, and promises. God later revealed the details of this covenant after Noah and his family left the ark (see 8:20–9:17).

What does God's initiative in establishing the first covenant tell you about His grace? How are you comforted by knowing that God has taken the initiative to provide a way of salvation for you?

Noah stood courageously for God in the midst of a corrupt society. Peter referred to Noah as "a preacher of righteousness" (2 Pet. 2:5). Noah spoke the truth even when it was unpopular to do so. Apparently, no one took Noah or his preaching seriously and no one repented as a result of his preaching. When God's patience finally ran its course, the first drops of rain fell from the sky. The drops soon became torrential and mixed with the waters that burst forth from the springs below to create an inescapable and cataclysmic flood.

The first raindrops signaled that the time of judgment had arrived. For years, men and women were convinced their actions had no lasting consequences, but no more. The rain signaled the end of God's patience and the execution of His justice.

The rain continued for 40 days and 40 nights. As soon as the ground became completely saturated, the water had nowhere to go but up. The waters continued to rise for "150 days" (7:24). The waters rose so high that they even covered the highest mountains (see 7:20).

God instructed Noah and his entire family to enter the ark seven days before the start of the rains (see 7:1,4). Yet again, Noah obeyed God and entered the ark with his wife, his sons, and his son's wives—a total of eight individuals. Although they did not know how long they would live in the ark, they trusted God.

Noah's experience in building the ark, waiting for the rains, and entering the ark was a test of faith. What are some examples of tests of faith Christians face today? How do these tests compare to Noah's test?

Noah and his family did not have to go out and gather the male and female animals of every species. God brought them to the ark (see 6:20). Once everyone was safely aboard, God Himself shut the door of the ark and, by so doing, also took responsibility for those who remained outside the door and would perish in the floodwaters. No one outside the ark escaped God's judgment. His mercy was found only within the ark. As the water rose, the ark floated. All the earth flooded, as God said it would, as an act of His judgment. Noah and his family, however, were rescued as an act of God's grace.

Read Genesis 8:15-22.

We don't often think about what life must have been like on the ark. We don't consider the noise, the smell, or even the constant motion of the boat on the water. Noah experienced it all, and he experienced it for more than a year.

Consider that year on the ark. What do you think the substance of Noah's prayers would have been like during that year?

Eventually, the rain did stop, just as God said it would. After the rain stopped, the waters began to recede over a period of several months, and then the ark came to rest on the mountains of Ararat.

Noah's time aboard the ark is framed by two commands from God. When the time of judgment was near, God commanded Noah and his family to "enter the ark" (Gen. 7:1). A little more than a year later, after the waters receded, God commanded Noah, "Come out of the ark" (Gen. 8:16). Although Noah sent out a dove from the ark to search for dry land, he waited until God affirmed that it was safe for him to disembark. His life illustrates what it means to trust and patiently wait on the Lord.

What, if anything, makes it hard to trust God and patiently wait on His guidance? What problems can people encounter if they act too early or fail to act after God directs them to?

The flood destroyed every living creature with the exception of the animals on the ark—God's provision for repopulating the planet with animal life. Noah patiently waited until God told him it was safe to take the animals out of the ark. Too much was at stake to risk disembarking early. A year earlier, the animals had entered the ark two by two (see 7:9). When they exited the ark, they did so "by their families" (8:19). This phrase suggests that the animals exited in an orderly fashion.

The first thing Noah did when he came out of the ark and stood on dry land was build an altar to the Lord. This is the first mention of the word "altar," a place of sacrifice, in the Bible. Noah took some of the clean animals and birds (see 8:20) and offered them as burnt offerings on the altar. This is also the first mention of a burnt offering in the Bible.

Noah's sacrifice was an act of worship. As the head of his home, he demonstrated for his family members the priority of worshiping God. His sacrifice was an expression of gratitude to God for bringing them safely through the flood.

"The LORD smelled the pleasing aroma" of Noah's sacrifice (8:21). This is an indication that He was pleased with Noah and found his sacrifice acceptable. We also tend to lean toward smells that are pleasing and distance ourselves from those that are not. To refuse to smell something shows our displeasure with that particular thing (see Lev. 26:31). Paul would later refer to the death of Christ on the cross as a "fragrant offering to God" (Eph. 5:2), an indication that God was pleased with Christ's sacrifice.

The Lord said that, in spite of humanity's inclination toward evil, He would never again curse the ground. Previously, God had cursed the ground because of Adam (see 3:17) and also after Cain murdered his brother Abel (see 4:11-12). Had God chosen to curse the ground again, it would have made it even more difficult for humanity to eke out a living. God's decision not to curse the ground and add to humanity's affliction was an expression of His kindness. The Lord also determined that He would never again send a universal flood as a form of judgment—yet another expression of His grace.

The cataclysmic flood had disrupted the normal rhythm of the seasons. While the floodwaters covered the earth, there was no seedtime and harvest—both essential for the sustenance of human life. Planting and harvesting, interrupted for the duration of the flood, are activities that are dependent on the seasons and the weather. After the flood, God affirmed that the seasons would return to their normal cycles. People would be able to plant, grow, and harvest the crops needed in order to survive.

ABRAHAM

The Man Who Followed God

INTRODUCTION

You'd be hard-pressed to find someone (other than Jesus) who figures more prominently in the Bible than Abraham. His story is referred to frequently by the biblical writers, and even by Jesus Himself. In fact, Abraham is so essential to Scripture that it's hard to understand many parts of the Bible without a basic understanding of him and his story.

But here, in the beginning, Abraham is just Abram, an aging and childless man who heard a simple call from God to go. Abram obeyed, and his story really began as he followed God in faith, waiting for the fulfillment of the promises given to him. These promises frame the entire biblical story, for from Abram would come the nation of God's chosen people, the Israelites. And in the New Testament, we find that Abraham's fatherhood extends beyond blood to all those who believe in the same way that he did.

The old children's song is right: "Father Abraham had many sons. . . . I am one of them, and so are you, so let's just praise the Lord."

Abraham spent much of his life waiting. Why do you think waiting is so difficult for us as human beings?

How does our faith impact our willingness and ability to wait?

Watch the video teaching for Session 3 to discover "The World of Abraham," then continue the group discussion.

GROUP DISCUSSION

FOCUS ATTENTION

Describe a time when your life was changed in a moment. How did you respond?

EXPLORE THE TEXT

As a group, read Genesis 12:1-9.

How does Abram's call of separation to leave land, culture, and family relate to the calling of followers of Christ? How do the promises given to Abram in verses 2-3 relate to us today?

What things get left behind when a person commits to following Christ?

As a group, read Genesis 15:1-6.

How was Abram justified in his faith? How is the justification that believers experience today through Christ the same or different from Abram's?

As a group, read Genesis 21:1-8.

What meaning do the words "at the appointed time" hold for Abraham and Sarah (v. 2)? What connections can also be made for believers in their walk with Christ in examining these words and their context?

As we reflect upon the climax of the story of Abraham, what made this moment so critical?

APPLY THE TEXT

God seeks people who will faithfully follow Him, even if that means leaving the comfortable. God's call requires us to act on our faith even while facing risk. This was true of Abraham, and it's also true of us. The blessing of God is reserved for those who demonstrate faith in Him through obedience.

What is God asking you to do that will stretch your faith in Him?

What roadblocks are keeping you from taking steps of obedience?

What are some practical ways you can encourage yourself or someone else to continue to wait for God to move and work in His time?

Close your group time in prayer, reflecting on what you have discussed.

ABRAHAM

KEY VERSE

Abraham believed the LORD, and he credited it to him as righteousness.

— Genesis 15:6

BASIC FACTS

1. Originally known as *Abram*, meaning "exalted father."

2. Son of Terah [TEE ruh], a descendant of Shem and also an idol worshiper (Josh. 24:2).

3. Childhood spent in Ur of the Chaldees, a prominent Sumerian city in lower Mesopotamia.

4. Left Haran at age 75 with his wife and nephew to settle in Canaan.

5. Fathered Ishmael at age 86 with Sarah's handmaid, Hagar; fathered Isaac at age 100 with Sarah.

6. Abraham died at the age of 175.

TIMELINE

4000–2000 BC

- Tower of Babel built 2250
- Job 2100–1900
- Abraham 2166–1991
- Mesopotamia 2000
- Eleventh Dynasty of Egypt 2134–1991
- Third Dynasty of Ur 2113–2006

2000–1900 BC

- Isaac 2066–1886
- Jacob 2006–1859
- Twelfth Dynasty of Egypt 1991–1786
- Chinese create first zoo 2000
- Code of medical ethics in Mesopotamia 2000
- Babylonians, Egyptians divide days into hours, minutes, and seconds 2000

KNOWN FOR

1. When Abraham was seventy-five years old, he obeyed God's call to move to Canaan, a land God promised to give Abraham and his descendants. God promised to bless Abraham by making his name great, making him the father of a great nation, and using his family to bless all the peoples of the earth (Gen. 12:1-3).

2. Abraham obeyed God's instruction to signify the covenant through the circumcision of all males in his family—both present and future (Gen. 17:23-24).

3. He interceded with the Lord when the wicked city of Sodom—where his nephew, Lot, and his family lived—was about to be destroyed in judgment (Gen. 18:22-33).

4. He obeyed the Lord's test of faith in being willing to offer his son Isaac as a sacrifice. God stopped Abraham from sacrificing Isaac, and He provided a ram as a substitute for Abraham's offering (Gen. 22:1-19).

5. Abraham occasionally faltered in his faith. He once claimed to an Egyptian ruler that Sarah was his sister, not his wife, because he was afraid the ruler would kill him (Gen. 12:11-13). Later, he and Sarah failed to wait on the Lord to give them a son, choosing instead to use Sarah's handmaid as a surrogate mother (Gen. 16:1-3).

6. In the New Testament, Abraham is remembered primarily as the forefather of faith-based righteousness (Acts 7:2-5; Rom. 4:3,11,13-16; Gal. 3:6-9; Heb. 11:8-10,17-19).

7. Today, Abraham continues to be remembered as a patriarch not only by Jews and Christians, but also by Arab peoples who descended from Ishmael, Abraham's son by Sarah's Egyptian handmaid.

1900–1800 BC

- Joseph 1915–1805
- Potter's wheel introduced to Crete 1900
- Joseph's mother, Rachel, dies during childbirth 1900
- Use of sails on boats in the Aegean 1900
- Mesopotamians discover what later became known as Pythagorean theorem 1900

1800–1700 BC

- Babylonians develop catalog of stars and planets 1800
- Book of the Dead, Egypt 1800
- Horses introduced in Egypt 1800
- Wood plows developed in Scandinavia 1800
- Hammurabi (Mesopotamia) 1792–1750
- Hyksos rule in Egypt 1710–1570

God's Covenant with Abraham

By Robert D. Bergen

God initiated the covenantal relationship with Abraham. God clarified the agreement through a series of divine revelations over the course of Abraham's lifetime.

This unique connection between God and Abraham begins in Genesis 12. The relationship began in Ur of the Chaldeans (see Gen. 15:7; Acts 7:2), some 220 miles southeast of modern Baghdad. In a gracious and sovereign act, the Lord communicated a series of authoritative commands and amazing promises to a man born and raised in an idol-worshiping family (see Josh. 24:2). Abraham had not been seeking any special association with God; the Lord initiated this Himself.

By the time the divine covenant had been fully developed between the Lord and Abraham—a process that took many years—both parties had performed several key actions. First, an initiatory act took place when the Lord summoned Abraham to separate from his idol-worshiping family and go to a place of the Lord's choosing (see Gen. 12:1). Second, a formal covenant ceremony took place. The ritual was solemn, mysterious, and significant. As part of the ceremony, Abraham slaughtered ritually clean animals and separated portions of their corpses into two piles. For His part, the Lord supernaturally caused a smoking firepot and a flaming torch to pass between the divided animals (see 15:17), thereby obligating Himself to fulfill covenantal terms. Third, Abraham and all males associated with him were required to be circumcised as a sign of submission to the covenant (see 17:11-14) and acceptance of Yahweh as their God (see 17:7). Finally, Abraham had to pass a test to demonstrate his submission to God. This test confirmed his willingness to sacrifice his son Isaac (see 22:9-12).

As part of the covenant, the Lord made several promises to Abraham. Most prominent was that Abraham, a married but childless man, would have many descendants. In fact, he would become the father of many nations (see 12:2; 17:4,16,20), and his offspring would be as numerous as stars in the sky and sand on the seashore (see 15:5; 22:17). Additionally, his descendants would include kings and tribal leaders (see 17:6,16,20). Although Abraham would have many sons, Sarah's son Isaac—the first son sired by Abraham after he had taken the covenant sign on his body—would be the primary expression of the covenant relationship.

Robert D. Bergen, "God's Covenant with Abraham," *Biblical Illustrator*, Fall 2015.

Second in prominence among the covenant promises was for a homeland. On five occasions (see 13:14-15; 15:7,18; 17:8; 22:17), the Lord promised Abraham that the land of Canaan, a region stretching "from the Brook of Egypt to the great river, the Euphrates River" (15:18), would be the lasting possession of his descendants, though it would not be given to them for many years (see 15:13-16).

Finally, God promised to bless Abraham and his descendants (see 12:2; 22:17). He promised to protect Abraham and make him famous (see 12:2-3; 15:1). God's covenant with Abraham brought blessings to the patriarch and his progeny. More than that, the divine blessing bestowed on Abraham was extended to all peoples (see 12:2-3) through Abraham's greatest descendant, Jesus Christ (see Matt. 1:1).

A Herodian building in a remarkable state of preservation erected by King Herod over the caves of Machpelah at Hebron in Israel. It is here Abraham, Sarah, Isaac, Rebekah, Jacob, and Leah were buried.

Illustrator Photo/David Rogers (4/11/2)

A 24-room house at Ur was reconstructed in the 1990s and dubbed "Abraham's House."

Illustrator Photo/ Philip J. Gaffney (32/2/6)

Read Genesis 12:1-9.

Abram knew exactly what God expected him to do, and it can be summarized in one word: *Go.*

Like Abram, we often have absolute clarity on God's will from the Bible. When we see God's clear word, we can obey or disobey. Abram had a clear word from the Lord. God wanted him to leave the land where he lived and go to a new land. Abram was faced with the decision of obedience or disobedience.

For Abram, this was a significant decision, and God knew it. To obey meant not only going somewhere, but leaving somewhere and leaving everything he knew behind. Furthermore, God required Abram to follow His direction without even knowing the final destination.

Try to put yourself in Abram's place. What are some of the ways you might have rationalized not obeying God's command?

What must Abram have believed to be true about God in order to obey His direction?

God not only issued the command, He declared some promises of blessings that would come with obedience. If Abram was willing to act in faith, then he would be the father of a great nation. He would be blessed, and his name would be made great. And in the end, every nation on the earth would be blessed through him.

Abram's obedience had worldwide implications. This was a history-shaping moment for who was, up to this point, a very ordinary man. But this is how the Lord works. God chooses to use regular, ordinary people who put their full faith in Him as conduits of His blessing even to the ends of the earth. Those great blessings begin with people willing to take God at His Word and step out in faith.

In Abram's case, this promise was fulfilled most fully in the person of Jesus. Jesus, born of the lineage of Abraham, is the means by which people of every tongue and tribe can be blessed with the greatest gift—eternal life. This promise to Abram foreshadows the coming of the Messiah, the one who would remove the curse of sin through the cross and bless with everlasting life all who trust Him. Through Christ, men and women can be set free from the bondage of sin and find the freedom that comes with salvation. The gospel message is the means by which all who are dead in trespasses and sins can gain eternal life through the Lord Jesus.

In what ways has Abram's obedient faith been a blessing to the world? In what ways can our obedient faith be a blessing to others?

Verse 4 begins with simple, but consequential, words: "So Abram went." Despite all the difficulties of following the Lord into the unknown, Abram obeyed Him. Simple obedience is the demonstration of our faith in the Lord. The text records this significant event as simple obedience to God's call. Without any argument recorded, Abram followed the Lord's command. As if to emphasize the gravity of the decision, the Bible tells us that Abram was 75 years old when he made it.

Rather than arguing with the Lord about the reasons he couldn't leave his home at the age of 75, Abram simply obeyed. All the blessings that followed happened because of this first step of faith.

Read Genesis 15:1-6.

We learn even more about the faith of Abram between Genesis 12 and 15. He left his home and followed the Lord to a land he had never seen (see ch. 12). He traveled to Egypt where God protected him and his wife (see ch. 12). His nephew Lot separated from him, but God continued to bless Abram (see ch. 13). Abram rescued Lot when Lot was taken captive by dangerous kings (see ch. 14). Through all of this, Abram continued a pattern of worship (see ch. 14). Abram, despite seeing God come through over and over again, still had not yet seen the child who would mean God's promise was actually starting to be fulfilled.

Perhaps God knew that after such a great amount of time Abram's faith was beginning to wane, and so He gave him the gift of this vision to encourage that faith. To do so, God described Himself as a shield.

How does God's description of Himself speak into Abram's current circumstances?

A shield was an important item in warfare in the ancient world. It was used defensively to ward off the blows of the enemy's swords or arrows. It could also be used offensively to strike an enemy at close range. God wanted Abram to know He was the shield that would protect him and enable him to fight and win the spiritual battles of life. What a comfort it is to know God protects us in the battles we face. He doesn't just send us out into the world and wish us luck. The Lord is our dependable defense.

Even so, Abram was frustrated over not having a son. There are moments in all our lives when God is, from our perspective, slow in action. For Abram, this perceived slowness led to a crisis of faith. Like him, we must decide whether we will trust the Lord even though circumstances and timing are not as we wish they were.

What challenges arise to our faith when God's timing doesn't line up with ours? What possible benefits might there be to a delay in the fulfillment of God's promises?

God's promises are not restricted by our timetable. God keeps His promises even though He doesn't always keep our schedule. That's why we can't only trust in God's ability to keep His promises, but we must also trust in His wisdom to know how and when to do so. God reaffirmed His commitment to Abram and even included a physical example. He pointed Abram to the stars in the sky—the very stars God Himself had flung into existence. Just as no one can count the stars, so also would Abram's descendants be without number.

We see the fulfillment of God's promise to Abram today. The Jewish people live in large numbers in Israel and many parts of the world, and those who have been adopted into God's family by faith in the Lord Jesus have become Abram's spiritual inheritance.

Then we come to verse 6. Despite all the evidence to the contrary, Abram believed the Lord. Is this not the essence of faith? To believe that which is unseeable? Unhearable? Even unimaginable based on our present circumstances? As he looked into the star-filled sky, Abram trusted that God was going to do everything He had said.

Abram's faith was "credited . . . to him as righteousness" (v. 6). Faith is the means by which we can be made holy and righteous before God. Righteousness only comes by placing our faith in our perfect Savior, who perfectly forgives through His death on the cross and resurrection. By trusting Jesus, we are made righteous and holy before God as though we never sinned.

How would you compare what Abram did to what a person does when accepting Christ?

Read Genesis 21:1-8.

Abram (having been renamed Abraham) and his wife, Sarah, followed God by faith into a new land. Years after the original promise of offspring, they saw God's promise fulfilled.

Though 25 years had passed since the promise was originally made, God kept His word. The Lord acted as He had said and did what He had promised. This is a strong reminder of the trustworthy nature of the Lord. We can trust Him because He is always trustworthy. He keeps His word and His promises to His people. He does not mislead us or fail us. While His timing may certainly surprise us, His faithfulness ought never do so. He is a God who can be depended on, because He is absolutely dependable.

Just as God promised, Sarah became pregnant and gave birth to a son. The Bible makes it clear—Abraham and Sarah were elderly. Imagine after the years of waiting, both before and after the promise came, what it felt like for Abraham to hold this child in his arms. It certainly wasn't the schedule they would have preferred, but it was, in the words of Scripture, the "appointed time" (v. 2).

In what ways could it have been advantageous for Abraham and Sarah that God waited 25 years to fulfill His promise to them?

In what ways can God's delay in answering our prayers be a blessing?

This child, the child of the promise, would be named Isaac. Maybe Abraham actually laughed himself as he gave his son this name, for the name *Isaac* means "laughter." His name would serve as a constant reminder to them that nothing is impossible for the Lord.

Abraham continued in obedience to God. In keeping with the covenant agreement, Isaac was circumcised when he was eight days old. It might have been easy for Abraham to consider his work done when the promise was fulfilled, but continued faith means continued obedience, and Abraham was not about to stop obeying the God who brought him this far.

How were the actions of Abraham a demonstration of faith in God? What is the relationship between our faith in and obedience to God?

Though Sarah previously laughed at the notion of having a child at her advanced age, she now laughed for a different reason. Her laughter now came from a heart overjoyed by the birth of her son. The fulfillment of God's promise brought a new level of trust in the Lord for Sarah. She found a joy she did not know prior to the birth of Isaac.

Perhaps the long wait made the joy all the greater. She lived for years without a child. She endured years of what must have seemed like endless waiting for a promise that had not been completed. She experienced periods of doubt in God's plan. But with the birth of Isaac, her joy overflowed.

Sarah's connection to Abraham caused her to think of his perspective. She noted how unbelievable it would have seemed had someone told her husband these events would happen. It seemed as though they would never have children together, and yet Isaac had been born. God provided in an exciting and amazing way. She was not the only one in the family rejoicing. They shared this family blessing together as husband and wife.

The lasting truth from Abraham's life is not so much about the faith of a man, though he certainly showed that. It's about the faithfulness of God. Indeed, the faithfulness of God is what inspires our ongoing faith in Him. We can believe like Abraham not because our faith is strong, but because God is faithful.

IV

ISAAC

The Miracle Child

INTRODUCTION

Twenty-five years is a long time to wait, especially when you are waiting for something very specific. But that's just how long Abraham and Sarah waited in faith for the beginning of God's fulfillment of His promise. Finally, after two decades, Abraham held his son, Isaac, in his arms.

What might Isaac's childhood have been like?

What might his mother and father have told him about God's promise and everything that happened before he was born?

Perhaps Isaac felt a measure of pressure being the child of the promise. Maybe he wondered what his own relationship with God would be like as he continued to live out the fulfillment of that promise. What found, even in the early years of his life, was that to follow God as his father had done, he would need to exercise the same kind of faith Abraham had.

Watch the video teaching for Session 4 to discover "The World of Isaac," then continue the group discussion.

FOCUS ATTENTION

What do you imagine the relationship between Abraham and Isaac was like? How do you think Abraham talked about his faith and God to his son?

EXPLORE THE TEXT

As a group, read Genesis 22:1-14.

What was the purpose of Abraham's test? Why might a test like this be surprising?

What do you think the conversation was like between Abraham and Isaac on their journey?

What connections can we make from the account of Abraham and Isaac to the cross of Christ?

As a group, read Genesis 24:1-17,62-66.

How did the servant show a proper attitude toward seeking the Lord's direction in finding a wife for Isaac?

In your mind, what was the time like for Isaac as he waited for the servant to return?

APPLY THE TEXT

Isaac's story is a story of continued faith, but more than that it's a story of God's provision. Just as God provided the sacrifice on Mount Moriah, He also provided a wife for the child of the promise. Because we believe in and follow the same God, we can trust that He is still the God who provides for those who trust in Him.

What do we learn about the nature of faith from Isaac?

What are some things you learn about God through tests of faith that you can't learn any other way?

In what area of your life is your faith being stretched most right now?

Close your group time in prayer, reflecting on what you have discussed.

ISAAC

KEY VERSES

Isaac said, "The fire and the wood are here, but where is the lamb for the burnt offering?" Abraham answered, "God himself will provide the lamb for the burnt offering, my son."

— Genesis 22:7b-8

BASIC FACTS

----

1. One and only son of the patriarch Abraham and his wife, Sarah.

2. Name *Isaac* means "laughter."

3. At forty years of age, Isaac married Rebekah, the daughter of his cousin Bethuel. Abraham arranged for a servant to find a wife for Isaac so that he would not marry a Canaanite woman.

4. Isaac received the same covenant promises God had made to his father Abraham.

5. After twenty years of a childless marriage, Isaac and Rebekah gave birth to twin sons, Esau and Jacob. Isaac favored Esau, while Rebekah favored Jacob.

6. Isaac lived to the age of 180 and was buried by his two sons at Mamre, near Hebron.

TIMELINE

2000–1900 BC

- Isaac 2066–1886
- Jacob 2006–1859
- Twelfth Dynasty of Egypt 1991–1786
- Chinese create first zoo 2000
- Code of medical ethics in Mesopotamia 2000
- Babylonians, Egyptians divide days into hours, minutes, and seconds 2000

1900–1800 BC

- Joseph 1915–1805
- Potter's wheel introduced to Crete 1900
- Joseph's mother, Rachel, dies during childbirth 1900
- Use of sails on boats in the Aegean 1900
- Mesopotamians discover what later became known as Pythagorean theorem 1900

KNOWN FOR

1. Isaac was a miracle child of God's covenant promise, born when his father, Abraham, was 100 years old and his mother, Sarah, was 90 (Gen. 17:17).

2. As a boy, Isaac became the centerpiece of a test of his father's faith (Gen. 22). God instructed Abraham to sacrifice Isaac as a burnt offering. When Abraham obeyed, God provided a ram—a substitute—to offer in place of the boy (Gen. 22:12-14).

3. During a time of famine in Canaan, Isaac considered moving his family to Egypt. However, the Lord instructed Isaac to stay in the promised land and trust in Him to fulfill His covenant promises. As a result, Isaac settled his family in the southern region of the land, first in Gerar and later in Beer-sheba (Gen. 26:1-6,23-25).

4. Isaac became a highly successful and wealthy herdsman. He also gained a reputation as a man of peace. On several occasions of potential conflict with Philistine herdsmen over water wells, Isaac moved his family and herds to a new place and dug new wells, trusting that the Lord would make him successful wherever he went (Gen. 26:12-33).

5. Like his father, Isaac faltered in his faith: He deceived some Philistine men in Gerar concerning Rebekah, saying that she was his sister, not his wife (Gen. 26:7-11).

6. In their old age, Isaac and Rebekah contributed to conflict between their two adult sons through favoritism. When Isaac sought to give Esau the all-important firstborn blessing, Rebekah and Jacob conspired to trick Isaac into blessing Jacob instead.

7. Isaac is remembered as an heir of the covenant promises and, therefore, a man of faith (Gen. 50:24; Ex. 3:15; Deut. 34:4; Matt. 8:11; Acts 3:13; Gal. 4:28; Heb. 11:9).

1800–1700 BC

- Babylonians develop catalog of stars and planets 1800
- Book of the Dead, Egypt 1800
- Horses introduced in Egypt 1800
- Wood plows developed in Scandinavia 1800
- Hyksos begin to rule in Egypt 1710
- Hammurabi (Mesopotamia) 1792–1750

1700 BC–1600 BC

- Body armor used in China 1700
- Minoans develop system of running water 1700
- Linear A script comes into use on Crete 1700
- Cookbook developed in Mesopotamia 1700
- Rhynd Papyrus (mathematical text) 1650

Isaac

By Ronald E. Bishop

Isaac was the child of God's promise to Abraham. In spite of the advanced years of Abraham and Sarah and her being barren, Sarah conceived and gave birth to Isaac. God instructed them to name the child "Isaac," meaning "laughter," a reminder of the joy he brought them, and of the fact each had laughed when God said they would have a son (see Gen. 17:17; 18:12).

Sometime later, God commanded Abraham to take Isaac and offer him as a burnt offering on a mountain in the land of Moriah. Allowing Abraham to bind him and place him on the altar to be sacrificed demonstrated Isaac's trust and obedience toward his father. However, Isaac's life was spared by God's mercy (see 22:11-13).

When Abraham's servant returned with Rebekah as Isaac's chosen wife, Isaac demonstrated trust in his father's judgment by taking Rebekah to be his wife. Further highlighting Isaac's character, he "took Rebekah to be his wife. Isaac loved her" (24:67). In a time when many men viewed women as property, Isaac's love for Rebekah was clearly genuine.

After Abraham's death (see 25:8), Isaac was the sole figure in the continuation of God's covenant (see 25:5). Like Sarah, Rebekah was barren. Isaac prayed; God heard his prayer and Rebekah conceived (see 25:21). Their two sons were Esau, whom Isaac favored, and Jacob, whom Rebekah favored (see 25:28). This favoritism eventually caused family strife.

Isaac demonstrated shrewdness and success in his dealings with others. Due to a famine, he settled in Gerar, where God extended to Isaac the Abrahamic promise. In Gerar, Isaac resorted to one of Abraham's tricks, telling the local men that Rebekah was his sister. The king realized Rebekah was his wife, yet did not banish Isaac as Pharaoh had done to Abraham (see 26:1-10).

Ronald E. Bishop, "Isaac," *Biblical Illustrator*, Winter 1993..

In Gerar, Isaac became a successful farmer (see 26:12-14). His wealth led to tension with the Philistines; ultimately, Gerar's King Abimelech requested that Isaac leave the area (see 26:15-16). Although conflict ensued, Isaac demonstrated humility and wisdom by resettling multiple times, ultimately and peacefully in Beer-sheba. There God renewed His promise to Isaac (see 26:17-25).

The issue of favoritism of Isaac's children came to a head when Jacob, Rebekah's favorite, tricked Isaac into giving him the blessing Isaac had intended to give to Esau (see ch. 27). As a result, Jacob had to flee to Rebekah's brother in Haran, where he remained for more than twenty years. When Jacob eventually returned to Canaan, he reconciled with his brother Esau and visited with his father again briefly before Isaac died.

Isaac demonstrated his faith as he honored God's covenant with Abraham. Isaac was successful in business, yet humble in his relations with others. Although a good husband, he had serious problems as a father. His and Rebekah's show of favoritism led to intense family conflict.

Isaac's life may seem uneventful when compared to that of Abraham and Jacob. Perhaps to say, though, that Isaac was the son of Abraham and the father of Jacob is no small epitaph.

Area of Gerar, Israel. Isaac went to the Philistine city of Gerar during a famine. There, Isaac repeated Abraham's mistake by passing off his wife, Rebekah, as his sister (Gen. 26:7-11).

Illustrator Photo/ Brent Bruce (126/B/1033) or (126/B/1035)

Read Genesis 22:1-8.

At some point after the birth of Isaac, God came to Abraham again, and He came with a test. In what might seem like a surprising twist in the story, God told Abraham to sacrifice his son. Remember how long Abraham had waited for this child. Remember that this child was the first stage of God's fulfillment of His promise to Abraham. God remembered these things as well, but He told Abraham to give up the very thing He provided for him.

Why would God command something like this? It was a test to prove the extent of Abraham's faith in God. Abraham had obeyed God before, and if he would do so again, it would not only show the depth of Abraham's faith, it would demonstrate how trustworthy the Lord truly is. We probably don't know the depth of struggle involved in a choice of obedience like this, but we do know the struggle to obey God in faith on a daily basis. Every time we choose to follow Him, we are testifying that we believe God is worthy of our trust.

Abraham resolved himself to obedience, and began preparation for the journey early in the morning. Amazingly, there is no indication of any hesitancy or doubt on the part of Abraham. After all, God had been trustworthy in all past dealings with Abraham. Abraham's faith in the Lord had grown immensely over the years. The donkey was saddled; the wood was chopped; and Abraham, Isaac, and two servants set out together.

While we often look at this passage from the perspective of Abraham, we can also view it through the lens of Isaac. We don't know how old he was at this point, but he was clearly old enough to express himself, and old enough to ask a few questions about what was happening. So what might the father and son have talked about on the long road to the mountain? Perhaps it was another chance for Isaac to hear the old stories about faith and God's provision. Or maybe it was an opportunity for Isaac to hear about his father's hopes and dreams for him as he followed God.

We do know that Isaac heard he and his father were going to worship, and perhaps the worship began before they got to the mountain. Every step forward was an obedient act of worship, and Isaac was along for the ride, watching firsthand what faith in action looks like.

When Isaac reflected back on the journey later, what might he have learned about the nature of faith from watching his father? How can reflecting on our experiences give us insight into both God and ourselves?

Abraham did not lose faith. He told the servants that he and Isaac would come back to them. Note the faith demonstrated by the usage of the plural. God had been faithful in the past, doing what seemed impossible. God was going to be faithful in the future, doing what seemed impossible. Though Abraham did not understood how, he knew that God keeps His promises and both he and his son would return—even if it meant God had to raise Isaac from the dead.

Though Abraham was confident, Isaac still had some questions. As they walked toward the mountain together, he finally asked the question that had thus far gone unspoken:

"The fire and the wood are here, but where is the lamb for the burnt offering?" (v. 7).

Abraham answered that God Himself was going to provide the lamb. Abraham could not have known at the time that God was going to provide another way—another lamb—for the sacrifice. Neither could he have fully understood at that moment that God would provide an ultimate sacrifice through the death of the only begotten Son of God—the Lamb who would be slain for the sins of the world. He only knew that God would provide. And that statement would ring true for Isaac not only on the mountain, but for the rest of his life.

What are some specific ways God has provided for you in the past? Why is it important for you to remember those specific acts of provision?

Read Genesis 22:8-14.

God provides for our needs. He sometimes provides in the everyday and usual ways. At other times God provides for us through miraculous means. The death of Jesus on the cross is evidence of God's glorious provision in our lives. Abraham did not yet know *how* God was going to provide, but by faith he trusted that God *would* provide. Isaac also took heart in the provision of the Lord; for he too would need that confidence in the moments that followed.

Remarkably, we don't get any indication that Isaac asked more questions or even struggled as he was bound and placed on the altar. We don't get the picture of Isaac crying out in fear as the knife came out and went into the air. For us, there is an incredible amount of tension building in this moment of the story.

Isaac was bound. The knife was raised. As it hovered in the air getting ready to plunge down, we see a very visible representation of faith in both the father and son. Abraham and Isaac show us that faith is not a concept; it's not an idea; and it's not merely agreeing with some general truths and principles. Faith and action are inseparable. Real faith inspires real action.

The Bible reminds us of the two-sided coin of faith and works over and over again. The Book of Hebrews teaches us that we cannot please God without faith (see Heb. 11:6). The Book of James points out that faith always leads to works (see Jas. 2:14-26). What we believe is demonstrated by the actions we take. This was true of Abraham and Isaac, and it is true of believers today.

What is the connection between Abraham's faith and his willingness to obey the Lord in his actions? How important is the connection between faith and works?

Just as the tension of the story reached its climax, the angel of the Lord called out to Abraham. Abraham replied to the Lord with an acknowledgment of His presence and listened as the angel of the Lord spoke the comforting words that Abraham was not to lay a hand on Isaac. The Lord told Abraham that he passed the test. Abraham showed that he feared God by not withholding his son. He demonstrated his great and unwavering faith in the Lord by his actions on the mountain. He trusted God with his most precious possession and followed the Lord completely, even in the most difficult circumstance.

We can trust God completely with all we have and hold dear. We can trust Him in the most difficult days and trying circumstances. Our faith is revealed not only by our words, but also by our actions.

What does it mean to fear God, and why is having that fear important? What does this test reveal to us about the nature of faith?

Not only did God spare Isaac, but He provided a substitute. Abraham looked up and saw a substitute sacrifice—a ram caught in the thicket. Here we find a shadow of a greater substitute that was to come.

Like Isaac, we are bound. We are not bound with ropes; we are bound with the cords of sin and death. Though we deserve death, God provided a substitute for us. Jesus is the substitutionary sacrifice for our sins. He is the Lamb who died in our place on the cross.

Abraham gave a name to this spot. He called it "The LORD Will Provide" (v. 14), a reminder that God provides as we follow Him by faith. We can trust His provision for our lives and for our future. God provided a sacrifice to take the place for Isaac on Mount Moriah. He provided His Son as a sacrifice for our sins on Mount Calvary. We can trust Him with all that we have and all that we are because His provision for our needs is assured.

Read Genesis 24:1-17,62-66.

As Abraham aged, he began to consider the future for his son, Isaac. Sarah had already died, and Abraham began to think about the kind of woman his son would marry to continue the covenant line. These weren't days when a father would necessarily consult with a son in choosing a wife, and we don't have any indication that Isaac would have resisted Abraham's making this choice. Even so, it was a careful choice to make.

Not only would Abraham want his son to be happy and fulfilled, he also was well aware of the fact that God's promise would continue through Isaac and his new wife. So he was clear—his daughter-in-law was not to be from among the Canaanites. This was because Abraham knew the Canaanites did not worship the same God who had been so faithful to him. He wanted to make sure that Isaac's wife would help him live in faith. So Abraham chose a trusted servant and gave him some serious and specific instructions. He was to go to Abraham's homeland to find this new wife.

What concerns might Abraham have harbored about the kind of person his son would marry?

Abraham's servant asked an obvious question: What was he to do if he was unable to find a woman from Abraham's ancestral home who was willing to leave her family and journey with him back to the land of promise? He asked if he should bring Isaac to her home if she was unwilling to come to his.

Abraham's answer was clear and gives insight into his understanding of God's purposes. "Make sure that you don't take my son back there," he insisted (v. 6). Isaac was not to leave the land God promised to his descendants. God promised this land to Abraham and his offspring, and Abraham was unwavering in his commitment to follow God's plan. Abraham was confident that just as God provided a son, and just as God provided a substitute sacrifice, He would provide a wife.

Though Abraham had absolute confidence in God's ability to provide, he recognized his own imperfect ability to read God's plan. After all, God's timing was very different from the expectations of Abraham. So, with a mixture of humility and absolute confidence in God, Abraham made his plans for the future of his son and future offspring. Isaac, meanwhile, played the waiting game just as his father had spent so much time doing.

What do you think prompted Abraham to tell the servant not to take Isaac back to Abraham's native land? What does his directive imply about the promises made to Abraham?

The remainder of this chapter in Genesis is yet another reminder that God will provide. He had already chosen the wife for Isaac, and He was clear in the way He answered the servant's prayers that Rebekah was the one He picked out. God led the servant to the right place, at the right moment. God orchestrated the travel and the timing to accomplish His purposes. God is sovereign; He knows our needs and is greater than our problems. He will direct our paths to accomplish His purposes as we trust and follow Him.

How was Isaac's faith tested as he waited? What do you think he learned about God when Rebekah finally arrived?

Philippians 4:19 reminds us that God supplies all our needs. It doesn't say God gives us all we want. We should be grateful that He doesn't—our wants are sometimes contrary to His perfect will. Just as God met the need for Isaac's future in accordance to His will, He will meet our needs as we follow His guidance.

JACOB

The Father of the Twelve Tribes of Israel

INTRODUCTION

God was faithful to Abraham, giving him the long-promised son Isaac. God was faithful to Isaac as well, continuing His promise of uniquely blessing this family so that eventually all the families of the earth would be blessed. Isaac fathered two sons—twins—named Esau and Jacob. Jacob's name meant "deceiver," and through the course of his life, he lived up to it.

Though he no doubt was aware of his family's special place in God's plan to bless the whole world, the story of Jacob shows us someone who was marked by self-reliance, envy, and favoritism. Yet even in the midst of his sin, God faithfully used Jacob for His purposes. God revealed to Jacob the necessity of faith and trust in God rather than in himself.

In Jacob, we see ourselves. We see our self-serving tendencies and our dependency on our own ingenuity and effort to try and manipulate circumstances for our own ends. But we also see the wonderful truth that God is not bound by our deficiencies. He not only uses us for His purposes, but He also loves us and is working for our good.

When have you desired for a good thing but gone about it in wrong ways?

How have you seen God use human plans to achieve His purpose?

Watch the video teaching for Session 5 to discover "The World of Jacob," then continue the group discussion.

FOCUS ATTENTION

Jacob's story is marked by self-reliance. Is self-reliance a good or bad thing? How should Christians view self-reliance differently than the rest of the world?

EXPLORE THE TEXT

As a group, read Genesis 27:18-29.

What are some of the specific ways Jacob worked to deceive his father? What's your impression of Jacob based on these verses?

What are some occasions in which you might feel the temptation to manipulate circumstances for your advantage? How does doing so display a lack of faith?

Look again at the blessing Isaac gave to Jacob by mistake. What sticks out to you most about this blessing?

As a group, read Genesis 32:3-5,24-32.

What do you think Jacob thought about the night before he was to meet Esau again?

Can you relate to Jacob in this? Have you ever felt like you were wrestling with God? What does doing so feel like?

APPLY THE TEXT

Jacob lived the first part of his life in a self-serving manner, convinced he had to be his own advocate. But after a true encounter with God, he emerged with a new identity and a new submission to God. The same thing can happen to us. Once we truly encounter God's power and presence, we too emerge changed, continually submitting to His authority and purposes in our lives.

What are some of the ways you see the impulse of self-protection alive and well in your context?

What does a surrendered life look like from God's perspective? What does a surrendered life look like from a human perspective?

How does the story of Jacob give you confidence in the character and purposes of God?

Close your group time in prayer, reflecting on what you have discussed.

JACOB

KEY VERSES

God said to him, "Your name is Jacob; you will no longer be named Jacob, but your name will be Israel. . . . A nation, indeed an assembly of nations, will come from you, and kings will descend from you."

— Genesis 35:10-11

BASIC FACTS

1. The second born of twin sons of Isaac and Rebekah.

2. Name *Jacob* is related to the Hebrew word for "heel." Can also mean "supplanter" or "trickster"; in other words, one who gains advantage over another by deceitful means.

3. Spent twenty years in Paddan-Aram [pay duhn – AY ram] working for his uncle, Laban. Married two of Laban's daughters, Leah and Rachel. Fathered twelve sons and one daughter with the two wives and their two maidservants.

4. Received the same covenant promises God had made to Abraham and Isaac.

5. Jacob died in Egypt at the age of 147.

TIMELINE

2000–1900 BC

- Jacob 2006–1859
- 12th Dynasty of Egypt 1991–1786
- Chinese create first zoo 2000
- Code of medical ethics in Mesopotamia 2000
- Babylonians, Egyptians divide days into hours, minutes, and seconds 2000

1900–1800 BC

- Joseph's mother, Rachel, dies during childbirth 1900
- Use of sails on boats in the Aegean 1900
- Mesopotamians discover what later became known as Pythagorean theorem 1900
- Joseph sold into Egypt 1898
- Jacob and family move to Egypt 1876

KNOWN FOR

1. Jacob twice cheated his twin brother to gain an advantage in the family inheritance. First, he convinced Esau to sell the birthright (as the firstborn) for a bowl of stew and piece of bread (Gen. 25:29-34). Second, Jacob and his mother tricked Isaac, his aged and blind father, into giving the patriarchal blessing to him instead of Esau (27:1-40).

2. Despite Jacob's deceitful ways, God chose him to be the heir of the Abrahamic covenant. Jacob first received the covenant promises in a dream at Bethel as he was fleeing from Esau (28:10-22). On his return twenty years later, Jacob wrestled with God (in the form of a man), and then received God's blessing. God also gave Jacob a new name—Israel—which can mean either "struggler with God" or "one for whom God fights" (32:24-32). This new name would later be applied to the Israelite tribes and eventually to the covenant nation (Num. 13:1-3; 2 Sam. 5:1-3).

3. Jacob was also the victim of deceit. He worked for Laban seven years to marry his uncle's younger daughter, Rachel. On the wedding night, Laban substituted Leah, his older daughter. Jacob had to work seven more years to marry Rachel (Gen. 29:16-27).

4. As a father, Jacob refused to take action when his daughter Dinah was raped by a Canaanite prince (34:1-7,30-31). He showed favoritism toward Joseph over of his other sons, prompting them to hate Joseph, sell him as a slave to a traveling caravan, and then deceive their father Jacob into thinking a wild animal had killed Joseph (37:3-35).

5. During a time of severe famine in Canaan, Jacob migrated with his entire family to Egypt at the behest of Joseph (now second in command in Egypt) and with God's blessing and promise that the Israelites would become a great nation there (46:1-7).

1800–1700 BC

- Musical theory developed in Mesopotamia 1800
- Multiplication tables developed in Mesopotamia 1800
- Babylonians develop catalog of stars and planets 1800

1700 BC–1600 BC

- Body armor used in China 1700
- Minoans develop system of running water 1700
- Linear A script comes into use on Crete 1700

Jacob: All We Know

By Fred Downing

Conflict plagued Jacob's life; yet he was an answer to prayer. When Isaac prayed for his barren wife Rebekah to conceive, God responded (see Gen. 25:21). While Rebekah was pregnant, the Lord told her: "Two nations are in your womb; two peoples will come from you and be separated. One people will be stronger than the other, and the older will serve the younger" (25:23). Jacob and Esau struggled within Rebekah's womb and wrestled during childbirth. As Esau was being born, Jacob grabbed him by the heel and held on (see 25:24-26).

A "divine reversal" occurred early in Jacob's life. Jacob took his older brother Esau's birthright through heartless exploitation (see 25:29-34), and gained his father's blessing through deception and lies (see 27:1-29). In addition to vividly portraying the sinful human condition, the biblical portrait of Jacob as a supplanter, trickster, and deceiver emphasizes another central point. The calling and spiritual vocation of Jacob, who became "Israel," did not rest in his goodness or merit but in the free and mysterious will of God. The Lord's stating that "the older will serve the younger" seemingly foreshadowed both when Jacob won the struggle with his brother and the fact that God destined Jacob to be the father of the Israelites.

After his theft of his brother's birthright and blessing, Jacob's life centered on two significant events: Jacob's dream at Bethel (see 28:10-19), and his wrestling with God at the Jabbok River (see 32:22-32). God appeared to Jacob at Bethel during the night, identifying Himself as, "the LORD, the God of your father Abraham and the God of Isaac" (28:13). God made several promises—Jacob's descendants would be many, he and his descendants would possess the land, all the nations would be blessed through Jacob and his descendants, and God would protect Jacob and bring him back to his homeland (see 28:13-16). When Jacob arose the next morning, he made an offering and a vow (see 28:18-22). Jacob's vow was not one of absolute faith and commitment, but it was a beginning.

Fred Downing, "Jacob: All We Know," *Biblical Illustrator*, Summer 1988..

What followed the Bethel experience was an extended exile in Haran. It was a time when Laban manipulated and exploited Jacob. However, Jacob continued his exploitive ways. He became wealthy (see 31:2), married Laban's two daughters, and fathered many sons (see 29:1–30:32). But Jacob eventually alienated his father-in-law (see 30:25–31:2).

Obeying God's command, Jacob set out with his family to return to his homeland (see 31:3-21). He departed, yet Laban followed in hot pursuit. A bitter argument ensued, finally settled with a covenant (see 31:36-55).

Next came a watershed event for Jacob. At the Jabbok River, he wrestled through the night with "a man" (32:24), whom Jacob later identified as God Himself (see 32:30). Jacob prevailed and did not release Him until he received the divine blessing (see 32:24-29). At daybreak, Jacob was a different man, marked forever by this struggle. He limped out to meet his brother, Esau; yet Jacob the trickster was now called Israel, from whom would come the nation bearing his name.

From northern Syria, terra-cotta figurine known as an eye idol; Chalcolithic period (about 3500 BC). Rachel stole the household gods from her father when she and Jacob returned to Canaan (Gen. 31:19). Many people believed such gods could aid in fertility.

Illustrator Photo/ GB Howell/ Louvre Museum (35/16/81)

At the Jabbok River; at the Jabbok, "Jacob was left alone, and a man wrestled with him until daybreak" (Gen. 32:24, CSB).

Illustrator Photo/ Kristen Hiller (37/0018)

Read Genesis 27:18-29.

Isaac was no less than one hundred years old and believed he was approaching death. In Old Testament times, a father's blessing was more than an expression of love. As patriarch of the family, the father's blessing was an official, binding transfer of the patriarchal line, along with a prayer for prosperity and superiority. Isaac's blessing also meant the recipient and his descendants would be heirs of the covenant God originally made with Abraham and extended through Isaac. Jacob wanted that blessing that rightly belonged to Esau as the older brother. Jacob deceived others and maneuvered his way into his father's blessing.

The kiss was a formal part of the giving and receiving of a blessing. Here, it marked the end of the ceremonial meal (also a formal part of the blessing), and the beginning of the spoken blessing. Isaac's doubts about his son's identity had been removed. How was Isaac so easily deceived? His preferential love for the older son led to his deception. He heard (see v. 24), tasted (see v. 25), touched (see v. 26), and smelled (see v. 27) what he was looking for—Esau. Because of his unrelenting favoritism, he believed because he wanted to believe.

What are some ways favoritism is manifested in the church? What are some of the consequences that result from favoritism? How can we prevent it?

Isaac blessed the wrong son. Most social announcements are dispatched in a monotone voice, void of passion. But handing the torch to the man he thought was Esau surely was different for Isaac. This blessing would forever change the destiny of his son. Emotionally charged, he painted a beautiful future for his son, using the words "you" and "your" eight times in verses 28-29. Specifically, Isaac asked God to bless his son in four areas: prosperity, power, prominence, and protection.

But the blessing did not go to Esau. In an act of deception, it went to Jacob. Although Jacob took what God had promised him, this deception was not God's doing. We cannot justify using deceptive means to obtain worthy ends. Jacob orchestrated these events. Because Jacob stole the blessing, it cost him dearly.

Did the end justify the means of Jacob's deception? Explain.

In spite of Jacob's deplorable actions, God was faithful to His promise. God's promises are unchangeable based on His divine wisdom. They are not reliant on our part, but on His absolute faithfulness. While Jacob's journey could have been more enjoyable if he had waited on the Lord, God delivered on His promise, as He always does. Because Jacob did things his own way, God sent him to the school of hard knocks. Along the way, God worked on breaking Jacob's selfishness.

What were the consequences of getting ahead of God? First, Jacob's brother was so angry that he determined to kill him. Second, Jacob ended up fleeing for his life. Third, his uncle, Laban, deceived him into working fourteen years for his wife Rachel. Fourth, his brother would become the founder of an enemy nation. Fifth, Jacob would be separated from his family for twenty-one years. Sixth, he never saw his mother again. Imagine how different life would have been if only Jacob had waited for God to work in His way, in His time.

God, always faithful to His Word, prepares His people so they can be recipients of His promises. God can bring to pass His sovereign purposes despite our selfish actions. Let Jacob's misery remind you to faithfully follow God, even when you don't understand how God can bring His plan to fruition.

What are some examples of God accomplishing His purposes despite a person's sinful conduct? What can we learn about God from those examples?

Read Genesis 32:24-26.

After twenty years in exile, Jacob was going home, which meant going back to Esau. Once he crossed the Jabbok River, he would enter the territory where Esau lived, so he began to make preparations for meeting his brother. First, Jacob sent messengers to Esau informing him of his plans. The messengers returned with news that Esau was leading four hundred men out to meet his brother.

The report of such a large number did not bode well. Jacob reasoned that Esau still begrudged his past behavior and planned to attack him. Consequently, Jacob split his family and livestock into two groups (see vv. 7-8). He hoped the slaughter of one group would appease Esau's thirst for vengeance. Then, the defrauded twin brother might spare the other group.

Next, Jacob prayed (see vv. 9-12). He identified God as the God of his father and grandfather, but Jacob's petition was not grounded in their relationship to God. Rather, he based it on his own experience with the Lord. He opened and closed the body of this prayer with God's previous pledges to him. He acknowledged his own unworthiness of God's kindness and faithfulness. Jacob identified his progeny and prosperity as evidence of these characteristics of God. Then he petitioned God for deliverance from his brother's wrath.

After he prayed, Jacob took pragmatic steps to pacify his brother (see vv. 13-23). He separated animals from his flocks and herds to present as gifts to Esau. He designated servants to drive each type of animal in separate groups. As each group met Esau, the servant was to tell him the animals were a gift from Jacob.

Do you sense from these verses that Jacob had changed much from the time he left Esau? Why or why not?

Just as Jacob met God during a lonely night in Bethel (see 28:10-22) after leaving behind an angry brother and disappointed father, Jacob faced another lonely night with a surprising heavenly visitor. Some theologians believe the man who wrestled with Jacob is a preincarnate appearance of Christ. Although the Scripture is unclear about the man's identity, this is clearly the Lord or one of His angels (see v. 30).

Jacob was in no mood for a wrestling match. He secretly escaped Haran so he wouldn't be confronted by Laban (see Gen. 31:20). Then, he developed a plan so he wouldn't fight with his brother (see v. 3-8). The last thing on Jacob's mind was a wrestling match.

If Jacob's opponent was God or one of His representatives, how could He not defeat Jacob? Make no mistake about it; the Lord prevailed in the match by dislocating Jacob's hip and causing a permanent limp (see v. 31). Jacob would not give up. Jacob doggedly held on with all of his might until the Lord ended the wrestling match with just a touch of His finger.

How does this passage characterize Jacob's life? How do you see similarities in your own life?

With the pain of a dislocated hip searing through Jacob's body, the wrestling match was effectively finished. All Jacob could do was hold on in spite of his suffering and plead for a blessing from his heavenly visitor. Quitting was not a part of Jacob's vocabulary. At Bethel, God had promised Jacob His blessings, and from a material perspective, the promise was fulfilled because Jacob was wealthy with flocks, herds, and servants. After wrestling with the Lord all night, Jacob discovered he needed more than material wealth. He needed God and His transforming work in his life. Jacob was unwilling to relinquish God's presence: "I will not let you go unless you bless me." True transformation leads believers to value and seek God's blessing above all else.

How have you experienced life change as a result of your faith in Christ? In what ways do you still need God to change you?

Read Genesis 32:27-32.

With his wrestling match over, Jacob learned the Lord wasn't finished with him. God gave him a new identity. Before God continued the transformation process in Jacob's life, He called for complete transparency from Jacob. Jacob would have to admit who he was and the condition of his heart.

The Hebrew name *Jacob* meant "deceiver" or "heel grabber," a reputation that Jacob lived up to for most of his life. By asking Jacob his name, God forced Jacob into admitting his true sinful nature. God broke and then humbled Jacob so that Jacob could reach his godly potential.

What He did for Jacob, God also does for believers today. As we humble ourselves and submit to God, He molds and shapes our lives.

What are the dangers of not confessing your past? How does honesty and humility open the door for spiritual transformation?

Most of Jacob's life had been a struggle with men. He cheated his brother, deceived his blind father, and outwitted his unscrupulous uncle. Always looking for the upper hand, Jacob prevailed against men by trusting in his own schemes.

Jacob's new name signified a new identity. Jacob was not the same man who left Canaan twenty years earlier (see 31:38). He would enter the land of blessing a changed man, a man now known as Israel. This new title would also become the name of God's people, the descendants of Jacob.

When encountering God and His transforming grace, believers are forever changed. No matter how badly we have failed Him before, God can give us a new identity. Empowered from on high, we can find purpose and joy by serving the Lord.

Broken and blessed by God, Jacob's destiny (as well as the destinies of those who followed him) would forever change. What was true for Jacob is still true today. When we submit to God, transformation occurs. Blessings follow those who make seeking Him their highest priority.

Recognizing he had encountered the Lord, Jacob named the place of his wrestling match "Peniel" (face of God), as a sense of awe and amazement swept over him. Having met God at Bethel (see Gen. 28:19) and Mahanaim (see 32:1-2), this marked Jacob's third spiritual landmark. With each heavenly visitation, Jacob renamed the meeting place, acknowledging God's presence and transformation in his life. Not only was God preparing Jacob for his meeting with Esau, God was also preparing him to become the father of the twelve tribes of Israel.

At Peniel, God spared Jacob. Jacob thought seeing God face to face would bring death, but instead it brought him a changed life. By renaming the location and memorializing his encounter with God, Jacob associated Peniel with his spiritual transformation.

What are some life markers for you? How can your spiritual lessons be memorialized so the insight gained will not be forgotten?

JOSEPH
The Forgiving Leader

INTRODUCTION

Jacob, the deceiver, had been renamed Israel. With his new name came a new identity, one that trusted in the Lord instead of in himself. But despite this new confidence in God, Jacob made similar mistakes as his own parents.

History often repeats itself, especially in family relationships. Just as Jacob's parents demonstrated favoritism between their two sons, Jacob favored Joseph, the son of his beloved wife Rachel, and he exhibited that favoritism by giving him a beautiful coat. Such an act may seem like a small thing, but Joseph's brothers understood the meaning behind the gift—their father loved him more than he loved them. The hearts of Joseph's brothers turned against their younger brother. Thus began the saga of Joseph, a life which reads like an elevator, full of ups and downs. But through it all, we read about a man who was committed to a life of integrity and faithfulness, and a God who can redeem even the worst of situations.

What are some of the patterns of both obedience and disobedience you have seen in the generations of characters we have examined so far?

Based on what you already know of Joseph, how do you think he was able to maintain his faith and integrity despite the challenges he would face in his life?

Watch the video teaching for Session 6 to discover "The World of Joseph,"
then continue the group discussion.

GROUP DISCUSSION

FOCUS ATTENTION

As we will see, Joseph's story is about God bringing good out of something bad. Describe a time in your life when you have seen something good come from something bad.

EXPLORE THE TEXT

As a group, read Genesis 37:5-11.

What is your impression of Joseph based on these verses? What kind of young man was he?

As a group, read Genesis 37:19-27.

Are you surprised the brothers' jealousy escalated so quickly against Joseph? Why or why not?

Put yourself in Joseph's place. What are some of the things that would have been going through your mind during this sequence of events?

When have you doubted that God turns all things for our good and for His purposes?

As a group, read Genesis 41:15-21,39-41.

What do you notice about how Joseph responded to Pharaoh? What does that reveal about his character?

As a group, read Genesis 45:1-15.

Joseph's dreams were coming true as his brothers bowed down to him. What must Joseph have believed to be true about God to respond to his brothers in this way?

Not only did Joseph forgive his brothers, he extended them grace. What parallels do you see between Genesis 45 and the work of Jesus?

APPLY THE TEXT

Joseph encouraged his brothers by explaining God's providence in sending him ahead to keep them alive. Only God could come up with a plan that would enable a great many survivors a way of escape from the devastating famine. While his brothers only wanted their younger brother gone from their midst, God overruled their selfish desires by raising up Joseph as their deliverer.

Is there someone in your life you are struggling to forgive? How does the story of Joseph encourage you?

What does the story of Joseph teach you about how to live while waiting for God to keep His promises?

What is one circumstance about which our group can pray that you would be faithful and wait for God to intervene at the right time?

Close your group time in prayer, reflecting on what you have discussed.

JOSEPH

KEY VERSES

But Joseph said to them, "Don't be afraid. Am I in the place of God? You planned evil against me; God planned it for good to bring about the present result—the survival of many people.

— Genesis 50:19-20

BASIC FACTS

1. Eleventh of twelve sons born to Jacob (Israel); first child born to Jacob's beloved wife, Rachel.

2. Around age 17, received a multicolored robe from his father.

3. Sold by his brothers as a slave and taken to Egypt.

4. By age 30—through God's providence—became second in command to the pharaoh.

5. Married Asenath [AZ eh nath], the daughter of an Egyptian priest, and fathered two sons.

6. Reconciled with his brothers, resettling Jacob and his entire household in Egypt.

7. Died in Egypt at the age of 110.

TIMELINE

2000–1900 BC

- Isaac 2066–1886
- Jacob 2006–1859
- Twelfth Dynasty of Egypt 1991–1786
- Chinese create first zoo 2000
- Code of medical ethics in Mesopotamia 2000
- Babylonians, Egyptians divide days into hours, minutes, and seconds 2000

1900–1800 BC

- Joseph 1915–1805
- Potter's wheel introduced to Crete 1900
- Joseph's mother, Rachel, dies during childbirth 1900
- Use of sails on boats in the Aegean 1900
- Joseph sold into Egypt 1898
- Jacob and family move to Egypt 1876

KNOWN FOR

1. As a young man, Joseph dreamed he would rule over his family (Gen. 37:1-10), which incited his brothers to plot to kill him (37:18-20). One brother, Judah, convinced them instead to sell him as a slave to a merchant caravan going to Egypt (Gen. 37:26-28).

2. In Egypt, Joseph became the slave of a military officer named Potiphar and was put in charge of his master's entire household. When Potiphar's wife tried to seduce Joseph and then falsely accused him of attacking her, Joseph landed in prison (Gen. 39:1-20).

3. Joseph gained favor with the prison warden and was placed in authority over all the prisoners. He interpreted the dreams of two prisoners, including Pharaoh's cupbearer (Gen. 40).

4. Two years later, Pharaoh had dreams none of his counselors could interpret. The cupbearer remembered Joseph and told Pharaoh. Joseph interpreted the dreams as a revelation of seven years of abundant crops to be followed by seven years of devastating famine. Pharaoh made Joseph his second in command, putting Joseph—at age 30—completely in charge of the Egyptian government (Gen. 41).

5. God used the famine years as an opportunity for Joseph to be reunited with his father and reconciled to his brothers. Jacob's sons were forced to seek grain in Egypt. In doing so, they had to bow before Joseph, whom they did not recognize. After a series of "tests," Joseph revealed his identity to his brothers and assured them God had orchestrated events for the survival of the covenant people. He then urged his brothers to bring their father and families to Egypt (Gen. 42–45).

1800–1700 BC

- Babylonians develop catalog of stars and planets 1800
- Book of the Dead, Egypt 1800
- Horses Introduced into Egypt 1800
- Wood Plows developed in Scandinavia 1800
- Hyksos begin to rule in Egypt 1710
- Hammurabi (Mesopotamia) 1792–1750

1700 BC–1600 BC

- Body armor used in China 1700
- Minoans develop system of running water 1700
- Linear A script comes into use on Crete 1700
- Cookbook developed in Mesopotamia 1700
- Rhynd Papyrus (mathematical text) 1650

Joseph: Ruler in Egypt

By Bryan E. Beyer

Genesis 37–50 focuses on God's presence in Joseph's life. Despite Joseph's brothers selling him into slavery, through circumstances only God could ordain, Joseph became second in command in Egypt. From that role, he saved his family from starvation, thus ensuring the continuation of God's redemptive purpose.

Authority Assigned

Pharaoh had dreams that none of his wise men could interpret (see Gen. 41:1-8). His chief cupbearer recounted Joseph's ability to interpret correctly his own dream while the two were in prison. Pharaoh summoned Joseph, who provided a credible interpretation of Pharaoh's dream and proposed a plan to save Egypt during the coming famine (see 41:9-36). Pharaoh was impressed and appointed Joseph to oversee the plan (see 41:37-46). He also gave Joseph the daughter of a priest for a wife (see v. 41:45), which strengthened Joseph's position in Egypt.

Pharaoh elevated Joseph in several ways. First, he told Joseph, "You will be over my house" (Gen. 41:40). Earlier, Joseph oversaw Potiphar's house (see Gen. 39:4); now he would oversee Pharaoh's. Second, Pharaoh told Joseph, "All my people will obey your commands. . . . See, I am placing you over all the land of Egypt" (41:40,41). Joseph would serve as Pharaoh's representative before the people. Pharaoh also gave Joseph his signet ring (see 41:42). This ring imprinted the king's seal on a document and conveyed that the Pharaoh's authority lay behind that document. Third, Pharaoh told Joseph, "Only I, as king, will be greater than you" (41:40). Pharaoh thus demonstrated his support for Joseph through promotion, title, and marriage.

Authority Applied

Scripture does not say whether Joseph served as absolute second in command or as second in command specifically over distribution of grain. Clearly, however, Joseph's position held much authority, for Egypt's survival lay in Joseph's ability to implement his plan. Three Scriptures particularly illustrate how Joseph understood and used his power. First, when his brothers traveled to Egypt to procure grain, Scripture states Joseph "was in charge of the country" of Egypt (42:6). Second, when Joseph finally chose to reveal

Bryan E. Beyer, "Joseph: Ruler in Egypt," *Biblical Illustrator*, Winter 2019.

his identity, three times Joseph stressed how God had put him in his position. God had sent him ahead of his brothers to preserve life, to establish a remnant and save His people, and to preserve Pharaoh's house and the people of Egypt (see 45:5-8). Finally, when his father Jacob died and Joseph's brothers approached him afraid he would exact revenge for their having sold him into slavery (see 50:15), Joseph confessed his understanding of God's amazing purpose: "You planned evil against me; God planned it for good to bring about the present result—the survival of many people" (50:20).

Joseph faced many challenges; but in each instance, God showed Himself faithful. He preserved Joseph's life and used it to save His people, and thereby continued His redemptive purpose through Abraham's descendants. Joseph used his leadership position to serve those he led rather than to exalt himself.

Egyptian wooden model, painted, dated about 2000–1900 BC. The storage area in the back is divided into four compartments, each having its own opening in the top. Residents stored their harvest in these type compartments. They then retrieved the grain via the corresponding four openings in the front of the storage area.

ILLUSTRATOR PHOTO/ G.B. HOWELL/ LOUVRE MUSEUM (35/23/29)

From the temple at Medamoud, statuary head of Pharaoh Sesostris III, who ruled 1862-1843 BC, during Egypt's Twelfth Dynasty, likely during the time of Joseph.

ILLUSTRATOR PHOTO/ G.B. HOWELL/ LOUVRE MUSEUM (35/8/51)

Read Genesis 37:5-27.

Without the benefit of the written Word, God used a variety of methods to communicate with His people in ancient times. For the patriarchs, He often used dreams. In dreams, God told Abraham about the Egyptian bondage (see 15:13), and He promised protection and prosperity for Jacob (see 28:13,15).

Joseph, too, had a dream, and he shared it with his family. Upon hearing it, Jacob rebuked Joseph. Joseph's brothers were jealous of him. They envied their father's love and Joseph's divine dreams. Instead of being angry with their father, feeling excitement about Joseph's blessings, or using the occasion for self-examination, they jealously hated Joseph, and they waited for their moment to harm him.

When the day came, and Joseph was unprotected from his father in this faraway land, his brothers sprang into action. Not knowing for sure if their brother's dreams were from God, they wanted to make certain that they would never bow before him, even if God's plan called for Joseph to become a person of power. To cover their tracks, the brothers would tell their father that a vicious animal ate Joseph. Feeding on each other's hatred, their jealousy only grew more brazen as they acted out their devious plan. Sin, always loving company, turned the brothers into a ruthless mob.

Judah convinced his brothers that throwing Joseph into a deep cistern, where he would die of supposed natural causes, was a better alternative and would free them from a more grievous guilt. Although they did not know it at the time, what the brothers intended for evil, God used for good (see 45:5).

Have you experienced a time when your impure motives were used for good? Explain.

As soon as Joseph arrived, his brothers sprang on him, stripping him of the hated robe. Taking away his robe served three purposes. First, it would provide evidence that a wild animal killed Joseph. Second, the robe symbolized his father's favor; therefore, desecrating the robe was symbolic of removing both the one their father favored and his favoritism. Third, it signaled that they would never bow in deference, making Joseph's dreams null and void.

In an act of defiance, they threw Joseph into a dry cistern to die. Cisterns, or water wells, were deep with narrow openings, making it impossible for a prisoner to climb out unless someone threw down a rope. Joseph could not wrestle away from his stronger brothers, as they turned a deaf ear without mercy. Although he fought for his life, in losing the life he had known, Joseph would find an even greater life—a life in the will of God.

What Joseph's brothers did next defies imagination. They calmly sat down to eat a meal while their brother suffered and begged for his freedom. Poisoned by thoughts of jealousy, they acted as if nothing had happened. Judah would develop some fine qualities later (see 43:9; 44:33), but his motivation in talking his brothers into selling Joseph as a slave instead of leaving him to die was purely selfish. From his perspective, there was no monetary gain in letting Joseph die in the pit. They might as well line their pockets at Joseph's expense.

Though the brothers were motivated by jealousy and hatred, God delivered Joseph for a greater purpose. Jacob inherited the covenant blessings, and that made him and his descendants, including Joseph, special people in the eyes of God.

God can overcome people's evil intentions, turning the effects of those intentions for His good purposes. In the face of adversity, endure hardships with joy, knowing that God's plans will ultimately be accomplished.

How does knowing God is in control give you endurance to face opposition and jealousy from others?

Read Genesis 41:15-40.

Joseph had been thrown in a pit, sold into slavery, falsely accused of a crime, thrown into prison, and forgotten by everyone but God. Despite these circumstances, God had not abandoned Joseph, and he eventually found himself face to face with the most powerful man in the world. Pharaoh had a dream he could interpret.

Pharaoh shared with Joseph two dreams he had, and Joseph revealed that Pharaoh's two dreams meant the same thing—God was warning the ruler about an upcoming seven years of abundant harvest followed by seven years of famine. The fact that God gave two dreams meant it would happen soon (see vv. 25-32).

We learn several things from this interaction between the prisoner and the ruler. First, the world's wisdom, as wise as it may seem, doesn't have all the answers. Some things cannot be explained or discovered by human intervention. Second, in times of adversity, we must keep on serving the Lord. In spite of the long delay in prison, Joseph never faltered in obedience. Sitting on the sidelines is not part of God's plans when we are hurting. Third, God rewards faithfulness. Because Joseph remained faithful, God blessed him with the interpretation of Pharaoh's dreams. Fourth, we can point to God as the source of wisdom when called on to address difficult situations. Refusing any credit for himself, Joseph gave God all the credit. By doing so, he introduced Pharaoh to the one true God. Instead of swelling up with pride, Joseph honored God.

Trusting God, Joseph boldly outlined for Pharaoh a plan for the next fourteen years, one that would sustain the land for what was coming. But there was a deeper truth at play here. The Lord would not only use Joseph to sustain the land, He would position Joseph for the future of His people.

It's encouraging that God sometimes places His people in key positions to represent His interests. Don't dread these divine opportunities; look for them and seize them for God's glory. After facing years of imprisonment, Joseph knew the worst Pharaoh could do was take his life. Even that would bring him into God's presence.

The same is true in our adversities. Being ambassadors for Christ is more than a title; it is a way of life. God's light always shines brightest when it's surrounded by darkness. Like Joseph, be courageous and faithful, representing God wherever He places you.

When representing God's interests, especially before unbelievers, what characteristics should you seek to display?

Since none of his advisors could discern his dreams, Pharaoh concluded that Joseph was wiser than anyone else in Egypt. Even a king, who possibly had no prior knowledge of the one true God, knew that His Spirit was upon the young man. Impressed with Joseph, Pharaoh made him the second highest ruler in Egypt.

God had equipped Joseph for this moment. The things Joseph endured at the hands of his brothers, as a slave, as a house steward, and as a prisoner, all prepared him for the task he was about to begin. Suddenly, all the lessons learned came together for Joseph, making sense out of the trials. Like Joseph, we can be confident God will equip us to accomplish His purposes in our lives.

How has God used your past experiences to equip you for His purposes and plans?

Read Genesis 45:1-15.

A devastating famine struck as Joseph predicted (see Gen. 41:29-31), creating widespread hunger. Hearing Egypt had reservoirs of food, Jacob sent his sons, hoping they could buy enough to outlast the crisis. After a series of interactions with his brothers, Joseph could no longer contain himself.

Not wanting outsiders involved in this tender family reunion, Joseph ordered everyone out. Unrestrained, Joseph wept so loudly that all those waiting outside the room heard him. The word translated "wept" indicates an overflowing of tears. Overcome with emotion, Joseph invited his brothers to come closer and explained who he was. Spoken not as condemnation, his words were for identification and encouragement. The family secret was a secret no more.

While not all situations are reconcilable, whenever possible, believers should be willing to seek reconciliation with those alienated from them. Reconciliation is a major theme of the Bible, stressing the importance of being reconciled with God. For this very reason, Jesus Christ came into the world.

Joseph realized God overruled the brothers' hateful attitude and malicious actions, working it all out for good. Four times Joseph stated God was behind all these events (see vv. 5,7,8,9). His brothers were responsible for Joseph's sufferings, but God used them as a means of bringing about His divine plan. As a result of this spiritual insight, Joseph could reconcile with those who mistreated him by offering love and forgiveness. God's will, not the will of man, is the ultimate controlling reality of every event.

Joseph had been away from his brothers for approximately twenty-two years. While he was younger than his brothers, his understanding of God and all that God does was much deeper. Knowing the famine would last five more years, Joseph realized his family would not survive without his assistance. Now was a time for action and for thinking long term.

How does your understanding of God's purposes help you forgive others?

Spiritually discerning, Joseph knew it really wasn't his brothers who were responsible for him being in Egypt. It was God. Joseph's revelation was his way of encouraging his brothers—not condemning them. Yes, they had done wrong and were guilty; however, Joseph didn't want them dwelling on their sins, but rather on what God had done for all of them. In His sovereignty, God had placed Joseph in a position where he was a father (advisor) to Pharaoh, a lord (master) over Pharaoh's entire household (his personal extended family), and ruler (governor) over everyone in Egypt. Without the brothers' realizing it, the Lord used them to fulfill His promised covenant with Abraham— that from him would come forth a nation (see Gen. 12:1-3).

Joseph's understanding of the bigger picture is the very reason he could forgive his brothers. God is always at work in ways we cannot see or comprehend. By faithfully trusting and serving Him, we can learn the lessons that God has for us even in the hardships of life.

How does looking at the big picture of life give meaning to your past hurts and injustices?

TIPS FOR LEADING A SMALL GROUP

Follow these guidelines to prepare for each group session.

PRAYERFULLY PREPARE

Review

Review the weekly material and group questions ahead of time.

Pray

Be intentional about praying for each person in the group. Ask the Holy Spirit to work through you and the group discussion as you point to Jesus each week through God's Word.

MINIMIZE DISTRACTIONS

Create a comfortable environment. If group members are uncomfortable, they'll be distracted and therefore not engaged in the group experience. Plan ahead by considering these details:

Seating

Temperature

Lighting

Food or Drink

Surrounding Noise

General Cleanliness

At best, thoughtfulness and hospitality show guests and group members they're welcome and valued in whatever environment you choose to gather. At worst, people may never notice your effort, but they're also not distracted. Do everything in your ability to help people focus on what's most important: connecting with God, with the Bible, and with one another.

INCLUDE OTHERS

Your goal is to foster a community in which people are welcome just as they are but encouraged to grow spiritually. Always be aware of opportunities to include any people who visit the group and to invite new people to join your group. An inexpensive way to make first-time guests feel welcome or to invite someone to get involved is to give them their own copies of this Bible study book.

ENCOURAGE DISCUSSION

A good small-group experience has the following characteristics.

Everyone Participates

Encourage everyone to ask questions, share responses, or read aloud.

No One Dominates—Not Even the Leader

Be sure that your time speaking as a leader takes up less than half of your time together as a group. Politely guide discussion if anyone dominates.

Nobody Is Rushed Through Questions

Don't feel that a moment of silence is a bad thing. People often need time to think about their responses to questions they've just heard or to gain courage to share what God is stirring in their hearts.

Input Is Affirmed and Followed Up

Make sure you point out something true or helpful in a response. Don't just move on. Build community with follow-up questions, asking how other people have experienced similar things or how a truth has shaped their understanding of God and the Scripture you're studying. People are less likely to speak up if they fear that you don't actually want to hear their answers or that you're looking for only a certain answer.

God and His Word Are Central

Opinions and experiences can be helpful, but God has given us the truth. Trust God's Word to be the authority and God's Spirit to work in people's lives. You can't change anyone, but God can. Continually point people to the Word and to active steps of faith.

HOW TO USE THE LEADER GUIDE

PREPARE TO LEAD

Each session of the Leader Guide is designed to be torn out so you, the leader, can have this front-and-back page with you as you lead your group through the session. Watch the session teaching video and read through the session content with the Leader Guide tear-out in hand and notice how it supplements each section of the study.

FOCUS ATTENTION

These questions are provided to help get the discussion started. They are generally more introductory and topical in nature.

EXPLORE THE TEXT

Questions in this section have some sample answers or discussion prompts provided in the Leader Guide, if needed, to help you jump-start or steer the conversation.

APPLY THE TEXT

This section contains questions that allow group members an opportunity to apply the content they have been discussing together.

BIOGRAPHY AND FURTHER INSIGHT MOMENT

These sections aren't covered in the leader guide and may be used during the group session or by group members as a part of the personal study time during the week. If you choose to use them during your group session, make sure you are familiar with the content and how you intend to use it before your group meets.

Conclude each group session with a prayer.

SESSION 1 | LEADER GUIDE

FOCUS ATTENTION

Share some ways in which you are creative. How does this kind of creativity imitate God's creativity? How is it different from God's ability?

- Everything we think of as "new" is really a recombination of existing ingredients. Though we may create a never-before-tasted combination of ingredients, we must first have the materials to begin creating.

EXPLORE THE TEXT

Ask a volunteer to read Genesis 1:1-5.

How is God's authority on display in these verses?

What attributes of God can we identify from the fact that He existed before the universe was created?

- God was, when there was nothing else. Both singular and plural references to God in Genesis 1 allude to the triune nature of God—Father, Son, and Holy Spirit. (John 1:1-3 points to Jesus being present and active during creation.)

- The Hebrew word translated "create" in Genesis 1:1 is only used in reference to God's work. This is a unique process that only God can do.

- God drew a distinct boundary between light and darkness. Light-dispelling darkness was a beautiful picture of Christ on day one of creation, and it remains so for us today. Day and night are creations of God that were spoken, and His naming of them asserts His rule over them.

Ask a volunteer to read Genesis 1:27.

How does the creation of man and woman in verse 27 speak to the inherent worth of every person?

- Only people are created in God's image with an eternal soul, spirit, intellect, depth of emotion, unique relational qualities, and the ability to reason.

- All people—regardless of age, health, mental acuity, or ability—possess precious, God-given worth, because they are created in His image. Because of this, Christians must affirm the value of every person in attitude and action.

Ask a volunteer to read Genesis 3:1-7.

What lies about God did Satan speak to Eve? Why do you think these lies are easy to believe and repeat?

- One of Satan's lies is that he's not all that dangerous, active, or even real. He is the master manipulator and deceiver, without mercy. To think we are immune to his schemes is naïve. We need to trust God's wisdom, power, and protection. Pride makes us assume we can successfully be our own god.

What do you think Adam and Eve hoped to gain by eating the fruit, despite God's instruction to avoid it?

- God provided the way for them to avoid temptation, but Adam and Eve chose not to trust Him. Their disobedience broke their relationship with God and brought spiritual and physical death upon themselves and all their descendants.

- Instead of the power and satisfaction Adam and Eve craved, they received the constant presence of fear, shame, and a sense of failure and inadequacy.

Ask a volunteer to read Genesis 3:14-19.

Sin must be judged because God is holy. How did God curse the serpent? Adam and Eve? How do you see evidence of these consequences today?

- The hostility Satan brought against Jesus would result in a death blow to the head for Satan. Though Satan causes trouble, his end is sure through Christ, the only seed of woman. God's redemptive love, power, and authority are on display.

- For Eve, pain and suffering in childbearing would intensify as a direct consequence. Children would then be brought into a world where death reigns. Adam's relationship with work changed drastically. He would be reminded daily of his physical frailty and continual journey toward physical death.

APPLY THE TEXT

Why is the story of creation central to a strong biblical worldview?

In what ways does the belief that God created humanity in His image impact your outlook on life?

How have you seen the sanctity of human life violated in the world today? What practical steps can you take to affirm that all people are made in God's image and are worthy of respect?

SESSION 2 | LEADER GUIDE

FOCUS ATTENTION

Summarize the story of Noah in one word. What does this man's experience teach us about God?

- Noah's story is a story of judgment. God, because He is perfectly just, will eventually judge sin for what it is. Noah's story is also a story of grace. Because Noah believed God, he was saved from His judgment. In the same way, God extends grace to all who trust in Him.

EXPLORE THE TEXT

Ask a volunteer to read Genesis 6:11-13.

How does God's judgment on sinful humanity during the days of Noah cause you to view the evil and corruption in our world today? How does it cause you to view God?

- We would do well to remember the power and holiness of God. Though His compassion is real and deep, His just wrath is real too. As the perfect God, He has the perfect right to judge sin, and does so in pure, unpolluted justice.

- Sin brings death to everything it touches. When we indulge in sin, we contribute to the sinfulness of humanity. God's people are called to purity, even as we walk in a corrupt society.

In what ways can considering God's judgment help us see His mercy more clearly?

- In Scripture, we see God always warning and giving opportunity for repentance before bringing judgment.

- Noah, "a preacher of righteousness" (2 Pet. 2:5), surely carried a heavy burden for his world when he grasped God's message. He knew the urgent certainty that sin would destroy all who didn't bow their hearts to God.

Ask a volunteer to read Genesis 6:14-18.

What beliefs did Noah indicate by his obedience to God?

- God gave exact instructions for the building of the ark, and Noah carried out those directions just as he was asked.

- God has made clear for us what He wants us to do through His Word. We are to know His Word and look to Him to lead us. Yielding our will and opinions isn't fashionable or comfortable, but to walk with God, we must practice obedience.

How is obedience to God different today than it was for Noah?

- In Romans 1:17, Paul stated, "The righteous will live by faith." This wasn't a new idea to the faith when Paul said it. Those who belong to God have always been required to walk with Him by faith, as evidenced by Noah and Abraham.

- Validation for Noah finally came when animals began to appear on the horizon. God asked Noah to persevere in obedience for a long time before he saw God's promise accomplished with his physical eyes.

How do the two promises in verse 18 relate to the rest of humanity and creation, beyond Noah's family?

- In Scripture, we see God always warning and giving opportunity for repentance before bringing judgment.

Ask a volunteer to read Genesis 7:7-14.

What does it mean to you that God keeps His Word, both in mercy and in judgment? What does this truth say about His character?

- Though He is patient and merciful, God is not permissive. He is perfectly consistent and trustworthy in His standard. God's commitment to perfect justice doesn't depend on emotions. He is never self-indulgent or manipulative.

- God's wrath toward sin is real, and everyone not protected by the blood of Jesus will be destroyed by it.

- We don't need to be fearful or paralyzed by the reality of God's judgment; we must consider it soberly and act on the urgency to pray for and share the gospel with others.

APPLY THE TEXT

What message does the account of Noah have for us today regarding obedience? The seriousness of sin? God's mercy? The importance of guarding and cultivating our hearts and the hearts of our family members?

What must Noah have been confident of regarding God in order to practice this kind of obedience?

How could that kind of confidence change the way you live in a practical way?

SESSION 3 | LEADER GUIDE

FOCUS ATTENTION

Describe a time when your life was changed in a moment. How did you respond?

- Life-changing moments often arrive unexpectedly and unexplainably. These changes help believers grow in their faith, because they realize their dependence upon God for direction.

- Abram had an experience that was life-altering for him. Living in a pagan society and worshiping pagan gods, God revealed Himself and His plans for Abram and His people in a powerful way. How Abram responded is a valuable lesson in the practice of faith for us as believers today.

EXPLORE THE TEXT

Ask a volunteer to read Genesis 12:1-9.

How does Abram's call of separation to leave land, culture, and family relate to the calling of followers of Christ? How do the promises given to Abram in verses 2-3 relate to us today?

- Abram's call is a reminder that God calls believers to trust in Him, even in uncomfortable situations. He knew the land, he was surrounded by family, and he had amassed wealth. God taught Abram that the blessings He provides go beyond those that are temporal (prestige, wealth, etc.) to those of eternal significance.

- As children of God, the promise and principles of receiving the blessings of God through obedience remain. While blessings can be the result of obedience, we should be careful not to be obedient solely to achieve blessings.

What things get left behind when a person commits to following Christ?

- When we become believers, we receive a new identity as children of God. This relates to how we think, feel, act, and the call to put off our former way of living and put on the righteousness of Christ (see 2 Cor. 5:17,21).

Ask a volunteer to read Genesis 15:1-6.

How was Abram justified in his faith? How is the justification that believers experience today through Christ the same or different from Abram's?

- Abram did not understand the exact mechanism by which the promises were to be fulfilled, and yet he still trusted in the Lord; thus, the Lord declared him righteous.

- Justification is the act of being declared righteous and innocent before God, based not on works but on God's grace and mercy through Christ's work on the cross. Because Abram believed God, God declared Abram righteous.

- Abram's faith is the same in that it is based upon the work of God. It is different in that our faith is based upon the work of Christ on the cross as the ultimate fulfillment of God's promise of the blessing for those under the new covenant.

Ask a volunteer to read Genesis 21:1-8.

What meaning do the words "at the appointed time" hold for Abraham and Sarah (v. 2)? What connections can also be made for believers in their walk with Christ in examining these words and their context?

- Just as God's grace was at work in this event, His work in our lives occurs at the right time to accomplish His purposes. As believers, we need to learn how to surrender to the timing of God and trust that His Word is true and faithful in all circumstances.

As we reflect upon the climax of the story of Abraham, what made this moment so critical?

- There were undoubtedly obstacles that stood in the way of Abraham seeing the birth of his son, but God overcame all of those obstacles and remained true to His word.

- Just as Isaac's name and circumcision were reminders of how God worked in Abraham and Sarah's lives, we need to hold dear to our hearts specific times when God's promises were fulfilled.

APPLY THE TEXT

What is God asking you to do that will stretch your faith in Him?

What roadblocks are keeping you from taking steps of obedience?

What are some practical ways you can encourage yourself or someone else to continue to wait for God to move and work in His time?

SESSION 4 | LEADER GUIDE

FOCUS ATTENTION

What do you imagine the relationship between Abraham and Isaac was like? How do you think Abraham talked about his faith and God to his son?

- Abraham no doubt had plenty of stories to tell his son about God. He must have told him about his call, God's promises, and how Isaac himself was the beginning of the fulfillment of those promises.

- From Abraham, Isaac must have heard and also seen what faith is and looks like. This would have been important for what was to come.

EXPLORE THE TEXT

Ask a volunteer to read Genesis 22:1-14.

What was the purpose of Abraham's test? Why might a test like this be surprising?

- God didn't tempt Abraham to do evil by sacrificing his only son. Instead, God used Abraham to prove the quality of the faith he had.

- All of the tests that Abraham experienced prior to this point were in preparation for this ultimate test from the Lord. It was God's way of showing the type of faithful obedience that is required of those who follow Him.

What do you think the conversation was like between Abraham and Isaac on their journey?

- In Genesis 12, Abraham was called to leave his past; now in Genesis 22, we see the call to sacrifice his future, his precious son. By sending Abraham to a place three days away, Abraham had plenty of opportunities to change his mind.

- We know from the text that Abraham did not tell Isaac he was the one to be sacrificed. But we also do not have an indication that Isaac struggled as he was bound by his father.

- God used this moment of decision as a test of Abraham's spiritual character. But Isaac also displayed faith not only in his father, but also in the Lord.

- Abraham affirmed earlier how they would return together after worshiping upon the mountain (see v. 5), which means Abraham expected another miracle from God to assert that they would return together.

What connections can we make from the account of Abraham and Isaac to the cross of Christ?

- God did to Christ what Abraham did not have to do to Isaac. (Read John 8:56.) Believers can live in freedom because Jesus laid down His life, becoming the Lamb of God for all mankind.

- With Abraham renaming the place Jehovah Jireh, this name takes on significance in Christ's death; it became the place where the Lord provided the ultimate sacrifice for sins.

Ask a volunteer to read Genesis 24:1-17,62-66.

How did the servant show a proper attitude toward seeking the Lord's direction in finding a wife for Isaac?

- Isaac's wife was not to be a Canaanite, not forced, and led by God completely.

- The servant's prayer was intentional as a priority. He did not find Rebekah and ask for her to be the wife. Instead, before he met her, he sought God's complete direction (see Matt. 6:33). His prayer was also specific. The servant, in wanting to remove any doubt about God's direction, asked God for specific conditions to be met (see Judg. 6:36-40).

- His servant's prayer was interceding for Abraham. The servant wanted his master (Abraham) to be blessed by the results.

In your mind, what was the time like for Isaac as he waited for the servant to return?

- Isaac has learned the value of faith. Just as the servant trusted that God would answer his prayer, so Isaac was able to wait in faith for the Lord to once again come through.

APPLY THE TEXT

What do we learn about the nature of faith from Isaac?

What are some things you learn about God through tests of faith that you can't learn any other way?

In what area of your life is your faith being stretched most right now?

SESSION 5 | LEADER GUIDE

FOCUS ATTENTION

Jacob's story is marked by self-reliance. Is self-reliance a good or bad thing? How should Christians view self-reliance differently than the rest of the world?

- Our culture honors self-reliance as a mark of mature adults. In a sense, that's true. However, self-reliance can be dangerous for the Christian, because we can easily forget that God is our true source of provision and blessing.

EXPLORE THE TEXT

Ask a volunteer to read Genesis 27:18-29.

- As Genesis 27 opens, Isaac was old and nearly blind (see vv. 1-2). Before giving Esau the patriarchal blessing, Isaac asked Esau to go hunt some wild game for a meal. Rebekah secretly listened and quickly hatched a deceptive plan where she cooked a similar meal, dressed up Jacob to resemble Esau, and had him steal his brother's blessing (see vv. 1-17).

- Although the plan was his mother's, Jacob eagerly went along. Being ambitious, Jacob's only concern was that he might get caught (see v. 12). But because his mother agreed she would take his father's wrath (see v. 13), he concluded that the reward outweighed the risk.

What are some of the specific ways Jacob worked to deceive his father? What's your impression of Jacob based on these verses?

- Isaac's vision was greatly impaired, and his body was weak. Jacob seemed confident his mother's disguise would fool his father. Although absent from the explanation in the text, wearing Esau's garments trapped Esau's body odors, making Jacob smell like his brother.

- Hunting wild game was a time-consuming process. Jacob attributed his unlikely speed to the Lord.

- Isaac sensed something was wrong and questioned Jacob four times. Four times Jacob answered with a lie.

What are some occasions in which you might feel the temptation to manipulate circumstances for your advantage? How does doing so display a lack of faith?

- Believers have no need to try and manipulate circumstances, because they can be confident God is working out His plan and working for their good. This knowledge frees us to act with integrity in any situation.

Look again at the blessing Isaac gave to Jacob by mistake. What sticks out to you most about this blessing?

- Isaac's most valuable possession was being heir to God's promises to Abraham. One component of those promises was that their descendants would gain ownership of Canaan. So Isaac called upon God to make the land productive.

- After stealing the blessing, Esau was understandably enraged. Jacob fled and once again tried to manipulate his circumstances to his advantage. After a number of years, he had to return to his home and face Esau.

Ask a volunteer to read Genesis 32:3-5,24-32.

What do you think Jacob thought about the night before he was to meet Esau again?

- Jacob separated his family and possessions into two groups in case his approaching brother still held a grudge. He also sent smaller groups ahead to meet Esau and present him with numerous flocks and herds as gifts. These preparations left Jacob alone after the sun set. His solitude offered him no rest.

- Jacob spent the night alone, consumed with thoughts of fear not only for his life, but for the lives of all those he loved. The text tells us that Jacob wrestled with an anonymous man through the night.

Can you relate to Jacob in this? Have you ever felt like you were wrestling with God? What does doing so feel like?

- Because Jacob spent most of his life wrestling with people, God came that lonely night in the form of a wrestler. After wrestling with the Lord all night, Jacob discovered he needed more than material wealth. Jacob needed God and His transforming work in his life.

APPLY THE TEXT

What are some of the ways you see the impulse of self-protection alive and well in your context?

What does a surrendered life look like from God's perspective? What does a surrendered life look like from a human perspective?

How does the story of Jacob give you confidence in the character and purposes of God?

SESSION 6 | LEADER GUIDE

FOCUS ATTENTION

As we will see, Joseph's story is about God bringing good out of something bad. Describe a time in your life when you have seen something good come from something bad.

- Joseph had a long and winding road to get to where God wanted him to be. His job was not to manufacture his circumstances, but instead to remain faithful and trust in the Lord's plan and purposes.

EXPLORE THE TEXT

Ask a volunteer to read Genesis 37:5-11.

What is your impression of Joseph based on these verses? What kind of young man was he?

- Joseph might have thought twice before sharing his dream with his family. He must have surely been aware of what his brothers already thought about him.

- Joseph's dream clearly foreshadowed future events (see Gen.42:6;43:28). The brothers' reaction, however, suggests that they did not consider the dream to be a legitimate revelation from God. Instead, they considered both his dream and what he had said to be the ambitious fantasy of an overindulged child.

Ask a volunteer to read Genesis 37:19-27.

Are you surprised the brothers' jealousy escalated so quickly against Joseph? Why or why not?

- The reaction of Joseph's brothers was from pent up frustration over many months and even years. While Judah didn't rescue Joseph, he did offer a compromise that might save his life.

Put yourself in Joseph's place. What are some of the things that would have been going through your mind during this sequence of events?

- Time would reveal that God's plans for Joseph had not ended, but rather that God was turning the effects of these evil intentions for His good purposes.

When have you doubted that God turns all things for our good and for His purposes?

- If we were to continue to read the rest of Joseph's story, we would see that after spending time in prison, and being elevated to positions of authority there, Joseph eventually came under the gaze of Pharaoh and was made second in command of all of Egypt.

Ask a volunteer to read Genesis 41:15-21,39-41.

What do you notice about how Joseph responded to Pharaoh? What does that reveal about his character?

- Joseph assumed God would give him the answer, and he was quick to give God credit for the answer. Though Joseph had been in prison for more than two years, his first response was still to turn to God as the source of his wisdom.

- After Joseph interpreted the dream, Pharaoh put him in charge of preparing for the coming famine, which was the subject of the dream. Joseph would effectively control the food supply for the entire kingdom in the coming years.

Ask a volunteer to read Genesis 45:1-15.

Joseph's dreams were coming true as his brothers bowed down to him. What must Joseph have believed to be true about God to respond to his brothers in this way?

- Based on his reaction, Joseph was ready for reconciliation with his brothers. Remember, this relationship had been estranged for around twenty-two years.

- In order to respond like this, Joseph must have been confident in God's love, His power, and His wisdom. He must have been resigned to God's fulfillment of His plan in His way.

Not only did Joseph forgive his brothers, he extended them grace. What parallels do you see between Genesis 45 and the work of Jesus?

- God not only extends us mercy; He also brings us into His house as His children. This is true grace. As believers, we can reflect on what God has done for us in Christ, and one of the effects of doing so is that we are willing to extend similar grace to those who have wronged us.

APPLY THE TEXT

Is there someone in your life you are struggling to forgive? How does the story of Joseph encourage you?

What does the story of Joseph teach you about how to live while waiting for God to keep His promises?

What is one circumstance about which our group can pray that you would be faithful and wait for God to intervene at the right time?

Isaac said, "The fire and the wood are here, but where is the lamb for the burnt offering?" Abraham answered, "God himself will provide the lamb for the burnt offering, my son."

GENESIS 22:7b-8

Whether you're a new Christian or you have believed in Jesus for several years, the people of the Bible have so much wisdom to offer. For that reason, we have created additional resources for churches that want to maximize the reach and impact of the *Characters* studies.

Complete Series Leader Pack

Want to take your group through the whole *Explore the Bible: Characters* series? You'll want a *Complete Series Leader Pack*. This *Pack* includes *Leader Kits* from Volume 1 - Volume 7. It allows you to take your group from The Patriarchs all the way to The Early Church Leaders.

$179.99

Video Bundle for Groups

All video sessions are available to purchase as a downloadable bundle.

$60.00

eBooks

A digital version of the *Bible Study Book* is also available for those who prefer studying with a phone or tablet. Some churches also find eBooks easier to distribute to study participants.

Starter Packs

You can save money and time by purchasing starter packs for your group or church. Every *Church Starter Pack* includes a digital *Church Launch Kit* and access to a digital version of the *Leader Kit* videos.

$99.99 | **Single Group Starter Pack**
(10 *Bible Study Books*, 1 *Leader Kit*)

$449.99 | **Small Church Starter Pack**
(50 *Bible Study Books*, 5 *Leader Kit* DVDs, and access to video downloads)

$799.99 | **Medium Church Starter Pack**
(100 *Bible Study Books*, 10 *Leader Kit* DVDs, and access to video downloads)

$3495.99 | **Large Church Starter Pack**
(500 *Bible Study Books*, 50 *Leader Kit* DVDs, and access to video downloads)

LifeWay.com/characters
Order online or call 800.458.2772.

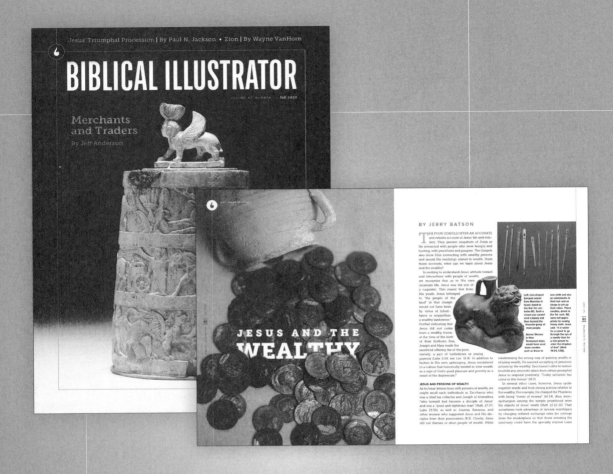

WANT TO KNOW EVEN MORE ABOUT BIBLICAL CHARACTERS?

The *Explore the Bible: Characters* series features information from the pages of *Biblical Illustrator*. And there are more insights on the way. Every quarter, you'll find remarkable content that will greatly enhance your study of the Bible:

- Fascinating photographs, illustrations, maps, and archaeological finds
- Informative articles on biblical lands, people, history, and customs
- Insights about how people lived, learned, and worshiped in biblical times

Order at lifeway.com/biblicalillustrator or call 800.458.2772.

Continue Your
Exploration

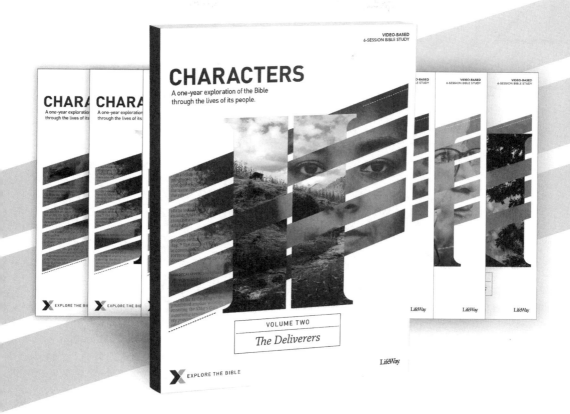

---------------- VOLUME 2 ----------------
THE DELIVERERS

Studying the characters of the Bible helps us understand how God works in the world, loves His people, and moves through His people to accomplish His plans. The next volume of *Explore the Bible: Characters* focuses on Moses, Joshua, Deborah, Samson, Ruth, and Esther. Build on your new knowledge of the Patriarchs and take a closer look at the lives of other Old Testament heroes.

Bible Study Book 005823504 **$9.99**
Leader Kit 005823536 **$29.99**

EXPLORE YOUR OPTIONS

EXPLORE THE BIBLE.

EXPLORE THE BIBLE

If you want to understand the Bible in its historical, cultural, and biblical context, few resources offer the thoroughness of the Explore the Bible ongoing quarterly curriculum. Over the course of nine years, you can study the whole truth, book by book, in a way that's practical, sustainable, and age appropriate for your entire church.

6- TO 8-WEEK STUDIES

If you're looking for short-term resources that are more small-group friendly, visit the LifeWay website to see Bible studies from a variety of noteworthy authors, including Ravi Zacharias, J.D. Greear, Matt Chandler, David Platt, Tony Evans, and many more.

Prices and availability subject to change without notice.